RELIGION IN EDUCATION

An Annotated Bibliography

TEACHER EDUCATION AND RELIGION PROJECT

EDITED BY A. L. SEBALY

National Coordinator

ACKNOWLEDGMENT To RELIGIOUS EDUCATION ASSOCIATION, 545 W. 111 St. New York 25, New York for permission to use reviews which have appeared in *Religious Education*.

RELIGION IN EDUCATION

AN ANNOTATED BIBLIOGRAPHY

COMPILED BY
JOSEPH POLITELLA

Kent State University

Kent, Ohio

AMERICAN ASSOCIATION OF COLLEGES FOR
TEACHER EDUCATION
11 ELM ST.
ONEONTA, NEW YORK

Religion in Education

First Edition

Church and education - bibliography
religious education - "

Library of Congress Catalog Card Number: 56-11992

PREFACE

The Teacher Education and Religion Project Committee of the American Association of Colleges for Teacher Education secured the services of Dr. Joseph Politella, Professor of Philosophy, Kent State University, Kent, Ohio, to compile and annotate this bibliography of *Religion in Education.*

It was through the foresight of Dr. Eugene Dawson, former National Coordinator of the Teacher Education and Religion Project, who saw the need, that this study began.

A work of this nature must be selective. Each reader will probably find references which he thinks should have been added. Admittedly some sections are stronger than others. Should this publication, however, stimulate further compilations and annotations in this field, and at the same time encourage study of Religion in Education, then the Teacher Education and Religion Committee will feel that the bibliography is serving its purpose.

For the reader's convenience the materials are classified into specilc subject areas. Where a book is out of print this is mentioned by (o.p.) . The reader should not limit himself to the classification of this text. A glance at the items will show that they have multiple use.

Miss Gertrude Rounds, Head Librarian, State University of New York, Teachers College at Oneonta should be given special recognition, and thanks, for the part which she has had in helping edit this publication.

Dr. Politella should be congratulated on the pioneer work he has done with a difficult field of endeavor.

Oneonta, New York, 1956.   A. L. SEBALY,
                                              National Coordinator

A PUBLICATION OF THE
AMERICAN ASSOCIATION OF COLLEGES FOR
TEACHER EDUCATION

Subcommittee on Teacher Education and Religion

Dr. John G. Flowers, President, Southwest Texas State Teachers College, San Marcos, Chairman

Dr. Evan Collins, President, State University of New York College for Teachers, Albany, New York

Dr. Eugene E. Dawson, Dean of Students and Administration, Kansas State Teachers College, Pittsburg, Kansas

Dr. Frank Dickey, Dean, School of Education, University of Kentucky, Lexington, Kentucky

Dr. Charles W. Hunt, Consultant, Central Office of AACTE, Oneonta, New York

Dr. J. J. Oppenheimer, Dean, College of Arts and Sciences, University of Louisville, Louisville, Kentucky

Dr. Gerald Read, Associate Professor of Education, Kent State University, Kent, Ohio

Dr. Harold K. Schilling, Dean, Graduate School, The Pennsylvania State University, University Park, Pennsylvania

Dr. Roscoe West, President, New Jersey State Teachers College, Trenton, New Jersey

Dr. Samuel M. Blumenfield, President, College of Jewish Studies, Chicago, Consultant

Very Rev. Msgr. William E. McManus, Assistant Director, Department of Education, National Catholic Welfare Conference, Washington, D. C, Consultant

Dr. Seymour A. Smith, Assistant Professor, Religion in Higher Education, Yale Divinity School, New Haven, Connecticut, Consultant

Dr. Kenneth I. Brown, Executive Secretary, William H. Danforth Foundation, (Ex-officio)

National Coordinator

Dr. A. L. Sebaly, Teacher Education and Religion Project, 11 Elm Street, Oneonta, New York

Executive Secretary

Dr. Edward C. Pomeroy, Central Office, 11 Elm Street, Oneonta, New York

FOREWORD

THE PURPOSES AND LIMITATIONS OF THIS BIBLIOGRAPHY

The purpose of this bibliography is to furnish the reader with an annotated list of commonly available books about Religion in Education. Books, which, in the main, express the Jewish, Protestant, and Catholic points of view. Reference, however, has been made to those volumes which connect Religion and Education in a broader non-theological sense.

From the compiler's point of view, Religion, it will be appreciated, permeates every aspect of life, even as does Education. For this reason some books are included here whose content and bearing may sometime seem remote from the ordinary notion of Education in its professional limitations. More and more is there evidence of the truth that every form of instruction premises for its background a certain view of man and his purpose of destiny. For example, even without being obviously didactic or with the intention of being moralistic, Literature reflects man's life and presumes something about man's aims in life. The various scientific disciplines, is so far as they are reflective along with being descriptive, presume certain connections between the life of men and the laws of the universe.

The temper of the times seems to demand that every study enter an account of how it fits in with man's needs, his welfare, and the direction of his growth. These considerations will explain the presence in the Bibliography of such books as Eddington's, *Science and the Unseen World*, DuNoy's, *Human Destiny*, and Weatherhead's, *Psychology in the Service of the Soul.*

The descriptions of the contents of the books are objective and positive. Occasionally the reader may detect evidences of the writer's personal enthusiasm. In all cases, however, an attempt has been made to present only factual information about the texts listed.

Some observers may object to the method of classification. An example might be: Where should writings about Psychology be listed? The writer chose Humanities. As good a brief could probably be made for its inclusion in Science.

This book obviously is not all inclusive. It is meant to provide suggested leads to further information rather than being a complete report. This publication should be considered as one among several working tools available to the reader in the study of Religion in Education.

The writer wishes to thank the librarians who have helped compile this materials, and the Teacher Education and Religion Project Committee, of the American Association of Colleges for Teacher Education, who have made it possible for him to compile these annotations on Religion in Education.

Kent, Ohio, 1956.   JOSEPH POLITELLA

CONTENTS

SECTION   I. THE GENERAL PROBLEMS OF RELIGION
             IN EDUCATION 1

SECTION II. CLARIFICATION OF THE SUBJECT 10

SECTION III. RELIGION IN THE HUMANITIES 22
             A. Philosophy 22
             B. Psychology 30
             C. The Study of Literature 35

SECTION IV. RELIGION IN THE SOCIAL SCIENCES 39
             A. Religion in Economics 39
             B. History and Historical Perspective 44
             C. Political Science and Government 45
             D. Sociology and Social Movements 49

SECTION V. RELIGION IN THE NATURAL SCIENCES 54
             A. Philosophy of Science 54
             B. Chemistry and Physics 56
             C. Connected with Various Aspects of
                Mathematics 56
             D. Biology and Zoology 57

SECTION VI. RELIGION IN PROFESSIONAL EDUCATION 60
             A. Principles of Education 60
             B. Childhood Education 63
             C. High School Instruction 70
             D. Colleges and Universities 72

SECTION VII. RELIGION CONNECTED WITH THE STUDY
             OF MORAL AND SPIRITUAL VALUES 79

SECTION I.

THE GENERAL PROBLEMS OF RELIGION IN EDUCATION

Allen, Henry Elisha. RELIGION IN THE STATE UNIVERSITY. Minneapolis: Burgess Publishing Company, 1950. Pp. ix 124. 2.75

A collection of papers read at a Symposium for state university administrators, faculty, and religious leaders of different denominations held at the University of Minnesota in 1949. The material is exploratory and probes into such subjects as the responsibility of state universities for meeting the religious needs of a student through courses of study and counseling, the legal limitations, trends of the day, and special problems.

Blau, Joseph Leon (editor). CORNERSTONES OF RELIGIOUS FREEDOM IN AMERICA. Boston: Beacon Press, 1949. Pp. viii 250. 3.00

For each of the essays, the editor has written an introduction. At the end of the text he has included notes and a general commentary. In the general Introduction, the writer seeks to clarify issues and to explain what "freedom of religion" means in its positive sense. It is pointed out that since 1787 the principle of religious freedom has often been under attack, but has never been overthrown. The editor thinks that in the U.S. at the present time, there is noticeably a trend toward the practice of freedom *for* religion and away from the individualism of an earlier day. There are selections of primary source material taken from various periods of American history: (1) "Colonial Stirrings" involves an appeal from Roger Williams (1644) and Wm. Penn (1670); (2) The "Wall of Separation" between Church and State is illustrated through Jefferson's "An Act for Establishing Religious Freedom" (1779); (3) and Madison's "On the Religious Rights of Man." Other noteworthy "cornerstones" include Z. Fuller's "The Tree of Liberty" (1830); and the keeping of religion out of politics; Horace Mann's "Religious Education" (1848); and Justice Frankfurter's "Concurring Opinion on the McCollum Case" (1948).

Bower, William Clayton. MORAL AND SPIRITUAL VALUES IN EDUCATION. Lexington: University of Kentucky Press, 1952. Pp. xv 214. 3.50

Bower's thesis is that though religious education is not allowed by law in the American public schools, society is endangered if there is lacking some kind of moral and spiritual direction to shape character. The early chapters of this volume deal with the historical background, indicating how the divisive influence of sectarianism and the

1

competition of rival church bodies to control public education led to the adopting of the doctrine of separation of Church and State. Later chapters deal with the development of the personality, the control of experience, the functional meaning of spiritual and moral values, and a program of instruction which reflects in some measure the Kentucky Program of Moral and Spiritual Values in Education. The Bibliography is very extensive, and brings together a helpful list of books on the subject.

Bryson, Lyman (editor), and others. FREEDOM AND AUTHORITY IN OUR TIME. New York: Harper and Brothers, (Distributors for the Conference on Science, Philosophy and Religion in their Relation to the Democratic Way of Life), 1953. Pp. 767. 6.00

Within the 767 pages, there are papers and comments on the subject by 75 scholars and teachers, mostly college and university professors. "Let the list of the six major divisions of the book give an idea of its comprehensiveness: 'Freedom and Authority, in Practical Life,' 'Freedom and Governmental Authority,' 'National and International,' 'Freedom and Legal Authority,' 'Freedom and Authority as Cultural and Social Phenomena,' 'Postulates of Freedom and Authority,' and 'Definition of Freedom and Authority.' "

Under these main divisions the contributors discuss the metaphysical backgrounds of freedom and authority; the dialectics of freedom; authority and freedom in industry, labor unions, international relations, culture, arts, poetry, education, government, law, science, morality. Opinions vary all the way from those of thoroughgoing humanists who interpret freedom and authority in terms of social evolution, to believers in a Supreme Being and a moral law and order ordained by Him. Ideas stretch all the way from empiricism to absolutism, from freedom to determinism, from reason to revelation.

"The contributors are earnestly concerned about the moral bankruptcy of Western civilization. They seriously seek for a solution congenial to their way of thinking. Some find it in the relativism of pragmatic philosophy, others in the physical and social sciences, while still others in orthodoxy. Between the white and the black at both extremes, one finds all shades of gray."

From the review by George P. Michaelides in *Religious Education,* XLVIII (Nov.-Dec., 1953).

Butts, Robert Freeman. THE AMERICAN TRADITION IN RELIGION AND EDUCATION. Boston: Beacon Press, 1950. Pp. xi 230. 3.00

Butts says that the purpose of the volume is to present the historical evidence that should be taken into account when teachers, school administrators, religious leaders, public officials and citizens make decisions regarding religion in education. The book presents material from original documents to help the reader to interpret the principle of the separation of church and state. He discusses "What Establishment of Religion meant in Colonial America," "The Principle of

Separation in the Original States," and the details of the meaning of "separation" in the nineteenth and twentieth centuries. The text is well-documented and should be useful especially for any who need to be well-informed on the subject.

Fleming, William Sherman. GOD IN OUR PUBLIC SCHOOLS. Pittsburgh, Pa.: National Reform Association, 1943. Pp. 248, 1.50

The writer of this volume takes a firm and positive stand, for the teaching of a non-sectarian religion in the public schools; for emphasis on character-building and education, in turning back the prevailing secularism and crime, and in restoring the fundamental truths of the Bible on which the founding fathers established the nation.

Hay, Clyde Lemont. THE BLIND SPOT IN AMERICAN PUBLIC EDUCATION. New York: Macmillan Company, 1950. Pp. xvi 110. 2.00

This book supports the thesis that "a type of religious education can be worked out which will entirely harmonize with the beliefs of Protestants, Catholics, and Jews, and which will at the same time be in harmony with the Constitution and the law."

Hullfish, Henry Gordon (editor). EDUCATIONAL FREEDOM IN AN AGE OF ANXIETY. New York: Harper and Brothers, 1953. Pp. 229. 3.00

This is the Twelfth Yearbook of the John Dewey Society. It contains eleven chapters by some of the most distinguished educators in America.

"This is a fighting book. The issues are: 'freedom of inquiry versus inculcation of fixed answers' . . . 'the right of individuals to decide from among alternatives vs. imposition on people of somebody's pet truth' . . . 'freedom of education vs. censorship of education' . . . 'the democratic method of intelligence vs. the authoritarian method of "telling them."'

The contributors are not neutral. They believe in freedom of inquiry. They believe in the right of individuals to decide from among althernatives. They believe in educational freedom. They believe in the democratic method of intelligence. They dislike totalitarianism in any shape. That includes communism. They believe that it would be tragic if in combating communism in this age of anxiety, our nation should embrace totalitarian means . . .

But this is not solely a partisan book. In keeping with the philosophy devoted to 'the values of democracy and the method of experimental inquiry' careful analyses are made of our situation.

It is a realistic book. It points up sharply the problem of education and of the public education in a pluralistic society in transition in which power to control is crucial. The dangers of a hysterical action because of anxiety are seen. It is a call to teachers to stand steady, to think clearly, and to act decisively under fire.

The chapter on 'Religion and American Education' by Philip Jacobson and Fred McLaughlin, and the one 'Military Training in

Education for Freedom' by Horace M. Kallen, will be especially interesting to religious educators.

"This is a mind-stretching, stimulating, well-written book. Even though one may not agree with all its conclusions it deserves careful reading."

From the review by Paul B. Maves, in *Religious Education*, XLIX (Jan.-Feb., 1954).

Johnson, Alvin Walter, and Yost, Frank H. SEPARATION OF CHURCH AND STATE IN THE UNITED STATES. Minneapolis: University of Minnesota Press, 1948. Pp. iv 279. 4.50

"The Christian holds no civil rights that the professors of another creed or no creed do not hold,"—such is the keynote of the book. Information is given in the preface that this volume is a complete revision, with additions, of Johnson's *The Legal Status of Church-State Relationships in the United States*, (1934.) The text should be especially useful to those interested in the litigations arising from an interpretation of the law as it now stands. In the various chapters, subjects such as these are discussed: Bible-Reading in the Public Schools; Released Time for Religious Education; Credit for Religious Instruction; Public Aid to Sectarian Schools, Extent of Parental Control; Free Transportation to Private Schools; Anti-Evolution Laws; Religion and Freedom of Speech, and other perennial issues.

Johnson, Frederick Ernest (editor). AMERICAN EDUCATION AND RELIGION: The Problem of Religion in the Schools. New York: Harper and Brothers, 1952. Pp. ix 211. 2.00 (o.p.)

This series of addresses, given at the Institute for Religion and Social Studies of the Jewish Theological Seminary, provides varied views on the role of Religion in Education. The editor defines the problem as: "How can public education, in accord with the function of putting each generation in possession of its full cultural heritage, do justice to the religious phase as constitutionally safeguarded in the First Amendment to the Constitution and in similar provisions in the constitutions of the several states?" The views represented in the addresses are widely varied. The first, a statement of the "Experimentalist" position solidly opposes and refutes the notion that there is a "common religious faith" which can be used as a point of departure for teaching non-sectarian religion. "A Jewish Educator's View" points out that while the fear of direct missionary activity intent on weaning Jewish children from their own faith is legally unwarranted, experience of the Jews has shown that such a fear is not altogether groundless. "A Catholic Educator's View" shows that "Catholics can never be content merely to cultivate a system whose aim is keyed no higher than to intellectual excellence cultivated in a religious atmosphere." The "Protestant Educator's View" is definitely committed to the notion that "these schools can and should include non-sectarian religious teaching as an organic part of their curriculum." Other chapters, which lend interest to the book are provided by educators who write on Religion in the

4

state university, in municipal colleges, state teachers colleges, private colleges, and in elementary and secondary education.

Lippman, Walter. AMERICAN INQUISITORS, A Commentary on Dayton and Chicago. New York: Macmillan Company, 1928. Pp. 120. (o.p.)

Lippmann's lectures, delivered at the University of Virginia, are concerned with the predicament of the modern teacher, under popular government, during conflict over religious fundamentalism and over patriotic tradition.

The same problem with variations presents itself to all whose business it is to popularize ideas. The Scopes Trial and the McAndrew case are taken as types of an ancient conflict between freedom and authority. As would be expected of Lippmann, the chapters abound with passages, cleverly conceived, reflecting on freedom and authority in clash and opposition. There is a Dialogue on Olympus where Socrates interrogates Bryan and Jefferson on their teachings; a Dialogue at Dayton between a Modernist and Fundamentalist regarding their views on the Bible and its interpretation; and a Dialogue at Chicago between a Scholar and an "Americanist" on the subject of loyalties. The third chapter has materials which are pertinent to the pressures which the community enforces on the teacher.

McCollum, Vashti Cromwell. ONE WOMAN'S FIGHT. Boston: Beacon Press. 1951. Pp. 221. 3.00

Mrs. McCollum became the central figure in one of the most publicized legal battles of many years; a fight, against religious instruction in the public schools, which eventually went to the United States Supreme Court. The account of her troubles is personal and human. One who reads it has the value of obtaining first hand information, which if not derived from the central figure in the controversy, is often colored and confused.

Mrs. McCollum describes her own views as "humanistic" and states that her objections to direct compulsory religious instruction, or that which results in indirect pressures, on the fact that such instruction often turns out to be indoctrination. The type of indoctrination depends on which religious group dominates the community.

Whether or not one agrees with the civic and religious philosophy of the writer, the text should be basic reading for anyone interested in the legal aspects of the case.

Martin, Renwick Harper. OUR PUBLIC SCHOOLS, CHRISTIAN OR SECULAR. Pittsburgh: National Reform Association. 1952. Pp. 152. 2.00

The functions of the public school increase in modern society. The attempt to exclude religious teaching departs from the historical function of our schools: to build sound character as well as to instruct. Modern secularism deprives the student of his birthright, the right to correlate his factual knowledge with religious knowledge and values

5

at the public school level. To this thesis Dr. Martin has dedicated himself. "Dr. Martin carefully reviews the McCollum Case. The logical results of such a case make morality a matter of secular interpretation to students, contrary to basic tenets of our culture. From what is added further, it seems that Dr. Martin's solution to the problem is not sufficiently specific to be helpful to everyone."

From the Review by J. Meade Letts, in *Religious Education*, XLIX (March-April, 1954) .

Nelson, Claud D. CHURCH AND STATE, A Guide to Study and Discussion. New York: National Council of Churches of Christ in the U.S.A., 1953. Pp. iii 39. .60

This discussion guide, on the subject of the interaction between Church and State, was prepared for the National Council of Churches. It is of special value for those involved in or desirous to be informed about the pros and cons of the controversy. Section I lists some 25 statements from individuals and organizations, reflecting views on the subject which range from extremely liberal to extremely authoritarian. Section II presents the history of the American Pattern. The final Section considers current practices or proposals tending to modify the American system.

Niebuhr, Richard H. CHRIST AND CULTURE. New York: Harper and Brothers, 1951. Pp. x 259. 3.25

This publication is concerned with answering the question of how far a Christian's life can be made to accord with his loyalty to Christ. The book attempts to rest the answer within the Christian faith. This writing then is concerned with the relevancy of Christ to the Culture of which a Christian lives.

O'Neill, James Milton. RELIGION AND EDUCATION UNDER THE CONSTITUTION. New York: Harper and Brothers, 1949. Pp. xii 338. 4.00 (o.p.)

The keynote of the book is contained in the quotation on the title page taken from the First Amendment to the Constitution of the U.S.: "Congress shall make no law respecting an establishment of religion, or prohibiting the free exercise thereof." The book, says the author, is offered in the hope that it will contribute to the solution of the problem of civil liberties. O'Neill writes as a Catholic layman, and as one well informed about the teachings of his church. "In this book," he states, "I am not arguing for federal aid . . . to parochial schools; I am not trying to justify Mr. Taylor's appointment to the Vatican; I am not defending religious education or 'release time' . . . . My position is that they are all debatable questions on which Americans differ with complete propriety; that they should be debated, cordially, factually, and decided by our democratic procedures; and that all Americans should abide peaceably, without rancor, by the constitutional provision and statutes which result from the working of the democratic process." The chapters of the book all reflect the postulates the author has set down, and present a very fair appraisal of the issues debated at the time the book was published,—e. g., the Everson Bus Case in New Jersey and the McCollum Religious Education Case. The Appendices to the book have valuable source material, such as the Bill of Rights, excerpts from the Supreme Court Opinions on the Everson and McCollum cases, and an essay "On Modern Intolerance" by James N. Vaughan. Particularly valuable is the well-chosen bibliography.

O'Neill, James Milton. CATHOLICISM AND AMERICAN FREEDOM. New York: Harper and Brothers. 1952. Pp. xii 287. 3.50

O'Neill, who is a teacher of argumentation and debate and chairman of the speech department at Brooklyn College, says that he writes as a layman, rather than a theologian, and that this book is written in defense of American Catholics who are accused as enemies of American Freedom. His book should be worth reading for anyone intent on understanding both sides of the case. He tells us in the preface that his book will meet the standards of being fair, informed, and accurate. The first portion of the book deals with the beginnings of American history, "The Framing of the Constitution" and "Catholic Support of American Freedom." In the next portion are discussions of such subjects as "The Separation of Church and State," "Catholic Education," "Catholics and Social Policies," and "Papal Infallibility." The part which follows is entirely refutative and examines the validity and sources of the statements and conclusions made by Paul Blanchard's *American Freedom and Catholic Power*. There are ten pages of excellent Bibliography, with a list of books and periodical articles dealing with the material which forms the core of the book.

Pfeffer, Leo. CHURCH, STATE, AND FREEDOM. Boston: Beacon Press, 1953. Pp. 675. 10.00

This large and scholarly volume is in the nature of a commentary on the words of an American jurist that "the manifest object of the men who framed the institutions of this country, was to have a State without religion and a Church without politics,—that is to say, they meant that one should never be used as an engine for the purposes of the other . . . For that reason, they built up a wall of complete and perfect partition between the two." "The purpose of the book," the author says, "is to examine how the experiment of the separation of Church and State came to be made as well as its implications and consequences." It has a very broad historical perspective, beginning with antecedents in Judea and Greece, examining the solution of the problem in various dominantly Catholic and Protestant European countries; and, traces the transplanting of the problems to the New World. An excellent survey of the aims and accomplishments of the book are given in the "The Ten Theses" at the end. This is one of the best sources available on court cases.

Stokes, Anson Phelps. CHURCH AND STATE IN THE UNITED STATES. New York: Harper and Brothers, 1950 (Three Volumes). Pp. lxxix 936; 799; 1042. 25.00

These volumes are among the best sources of materials about church and state in the United States. For the student seeking a general overview of the problem these volumes will prove invaluable.

Thayer, Vivian Trow. THE ATTACK UPON THE AMERICAN SECULAR SCHOOL. Boston: Beacon Press, 1951. Pp. x 257. 3.00

This volume is in many ways a defense of the principle of separation of church and state. The author finds the principle admirably suited to a country where there are multiple religious denominations as well as diverse religions. Religion is primarily an affair of the individual conscience, and freedom of religion requires strict neutrality on the part of the government. The writer states that the purpose of the book is "to review the evolution of the secular school and to weigh and appraise both the criticisms of secular education and the attempts now being made to revert to the old practices." For the reader intent on obtaining a complete picture of whether Religion and Religious instruction are permitted by our legal framework, this volume will provide a defense of the premises of the "liberal position."

Wroten, James D. EXPERIMENTAL DEVELOPMENT OF A COLLEGE COURSE IN CHURCH AND SOCIETY. Doctoral Dissertation. New York: Columbia University, 1951. Pp. 212.

"The purpose of the project was to discover the functional possibilities of the church in society . . . A college course called 'The Church in Society' was developed . . . at Millsaps College . . . Twenty-three students chose to make the experiment with the author . . . The author and students chose to use the democratic discussion method . . ."
"The class made a questionnaire (on issues—Race Problems, Crime, Alcohol, Community Relations, Leisure) to be taken to the churches throughout Mississippi, seeking to determine what the church was doing in society. Comparisons were made between what the class thought the church should do in society and what they found the church doing. From this came suggestions for improvement of the church's role in society. Some experiments for improvements were carried on by members who were ministers of churches . . . The democratic process makes possible the formation and development of ideas and attitudes to a degree that cannot be reached in the lecture type course."
Quoted from Helen F. Spaulding, "Abstracts of Doctoral Dissertations in Religious Education, 1950-1" *Religious Education*, XLVII (1952, 208-231) .

Yale University Divinity School. RELIGION IN STATE TEACHERS COLLEGES. New Haven: Yale Divinity School, 1952. Pp. 39.

This 39-page booklet contains a report of the conference on "Religion in the State Teachers Colleges" held at the Yale Divinity School, December 1951. There are reports of the findings of the study workshops on such subjects as: legal problems, religious courses, religious activities, relation of religion to other disciplines, chapel, moral and spiritual values in public schools, solving ethical and social problems through religion and others. There is also the digest of an address by Dr. Clarence Shedd on "Some Proposals for Religion in State Teachers Colleges."

CLARIFICATION OF THE SUBJECT

Bower, William Clayton. CHURCH AND STATE IN EDUCATION. Chicago: The University of Chicago Press, 1944. Pp. iv 103. 1.00 (o.p.)

The contents of this book are the expansions of a lecture given earlier at the University of Virginia. While much of the urgency of the problem brought out in the book has been dealt with in recent years and some solutions and suggestions advanced, the ideas of the writer will prove of perennial interest. At the back of the book there is a selected bibliography.

Brinton, Howard Haines. QUAKER EDUCATION IN THEORY AND PRACTICE. Wallingford, Pa.: Pendle Hill, 1949. Pp. viii 114. 1.00

It is evident from the contents of this little book that the clearcut philosophy of education worked out by the Society of Friends was based solidly on its religious faith and practice. The pronounced emphasis on history and the historical approach to the subject enables "the present to learn from the past not by imitating it but by cherishing the original intention which inspired it." The work is closely reasoned and thought out. Says the writer: "Nothing less than a complete philosophy of life is required in order to define education's purpose."

Brinton brings to his subject not only his knowledge of the Quaker community and its ideals of life, but a broad culture and refinement. He portrays the Quaker educational ideal as both religious and eclectic, and notes that the ideal for Friends' schools has been "The cultivation of sensitivity to the still small voice, willingness to obey it, and the practice of ways of living which enlarge inner dimensions of the soul . . ." In the main, the author stresses that Quaker education must emphasize an education that puts weight on authority in childhood, on the rational in youth, and on the mystical in maturity. True education cannot be separated from religion, and growth means growth in the direction of the realization of Life's purpose.

Brown, Kenneth Irving. NOT MINDS ALONE, Some Frontiers of Christian Education. New York: Harper and Brothers, 1954. Pp. 206. 3.00

"Using the term 'Christian' in a broad sense—as embracing the goals of both Jewish and Christian faiths in the cultural traditions of America—the author appeals for the recovery of religious values as an indispensable factor in educating the whole person." The executive director of the Danforth Foundation here voices the view, also, that unless American education can be brought to a deeper appreciation of the place of ethical and religious values, for both the teacher and the student, it will continue to fail its high objective. "When education becomes partial, provincial and dwarfed, the consequences are blindness and confusion." We are assured that the term "Christian" is used in no sectarian sense, but chosen for use in place of "religious" because it is more in accord with American cultural tradition. Two dangers considered are those of materialism and humanism—each of which divorces education from religious goals. There are some very instructive chapters, such as "Can Education be Meaningfully Christian?" "The Terrible Responsibility of the Teacher," and "The Measure of a Christian College."

Brubacher, John Seiler. MODERN PHILOSOPHIES OF EDUCATION. New York: McGraw-Hill Book Company, Inc., 1950. (second edition). Pp. ix 349. 5.00

Chapter XIII of this book is devoted to "Religious and Moral Education" with an elaboration of the view of *secularism* as a philosophy of education and spiritual values, humanistic religious education, and supernatural religious education. Consideration is given also to explaining Sin, Regeneration, and Grace, in Supernatural Religious Education.

The remainder of the volume provides an extended treatment of the educational philosophies prevailing today. It is scholarly and well documented.

Butterfield, Herbert. CHRISTIANITY AND HISTORY. New York: Charles Scribner's and Sons, 1949. Pp. vi 146. 2.75

The material for this book was originally presented as a series of lectures over the BBC. The material was then revised and presented in its present form. It is concerned with the meaning of life within Christianity.

Connell, Francis Jeremiah. MORALS IN POLITICS AND PROFESSIONS, A Guide for Catholics in Public Life. Westminster, Maryland: Newman Bookshop, 1946. Pp. vi 187. 2.50

This volume was written for the guidance of Roman Catholics who occupy positions of authority and influence in the community—public officials, judges, soldier or sailor, policeman, lawyer, doctor, and the rest. A separate chapter (xii) is devoted to the "Catholic Public School Teacher" which reflects in general the Church's philosophy of education and the personal ethics expected of the teacher.

Cunningham, William Francis. THE PIVOTAL PROBLEMS OF EDUCATION, An Introduction to the Christian Philosophy of Education. New York: Macmillan Company, 1940. Pp. xix 588. 5.00

Pivotal Problems of Education is a textbook which the author has used successfully with graduate and under-graduate students. It provides an extensive foundation in the subject, dealing with the nature of man, giving much attention to man's phychological and social needs, and examining four basic philosophies of education,—Idealism, Materialism, Humanism, and Supernaturalism. There are excellent supplementary booklists with brief descriptions of each at the end of every chapter. The list of forty-eight definitions of education (p. 18ff) provides a basis for comparison of various philosophical ends in education. Especially helpful and informative are the chapters on "The Education of the Teacher," "Rights and Duties in Education," and "The Philosophy of Catholic Education." "Education" says the author, "concerns the whole man, a mind-body organism, living in a material environment, a social environment . . . and an environment which is spiritual (God's providence)."

Dawson, Joseph M. AMERICA'S WAY IN CHURCH, STATE, AND SOCIETY. New York: Macmillan Company, 1953. Pp. 189. 2.50

Dawson makes a brief for the complete separation of church and state in order for religion to keep its strength. An attempt is made to evaluate the development of the principle of separation of church and state and what it has meant to the culture of the United States. He views the primary task of the church as one involving the creation of a religious society. Christianity's relationship, in the United States, to such topics as education, labor, and marriage, is discussed.

Dracher, Norman. THE INFLUENCE OF SECTARIANISM, Non-Sectarianism, and Secularism upon the Public Schools of Detroit and the University of Michigan, 1837-1900. A doctoral dissertation, University of Michigan, 1951. Pp. 171.

"The study examines the legal structure of the state as it pertained to the relationships of religion and education . . .
The records of the Detroit Board of Education, the University of Michigan, the superintendent of public instruction and other contemporary sources reveal that educational practices associated with religious aims were often so much more firmly rooted than constitutional restrictions, that a religious, often Protestant influence continued to prevail in public education.
. . . The public school withstood the powerful pressures of religious groups and succeeded in finding in secularism a formula for survival and growth."
From Helen F. Spaulding, "Abstracts of Doctoral Dissertations in Religious Education," 1950-1. *Religious Education,* XLVII (1952, pp. 208-31).

ENCYCLICAL LETTER OF POPE PIUS XI ON THE CHRISTIAN EDUCATION OF YOUTH. The Official Vatican Text. Derby, New York: Daughters of St. Paul, n. d., 1929. Pp. 56. (This publication can also be obtained from American Press, 70 East 45 Street, New York, 17, N. Y.).

This encyclical letter of Pope Pius XI contains and elaborates upon the philosophy of education of the Roman Catholic Church. Education, it emphasizes, is primarily a social activity, but a distinction is made between a type of education proper in "the natural order" including the family and society, from a type of education directed by the Church and representing "the supernatural order." "The proper and immediate end of Christian education is to co-operate with divine Grace . . . and takes in the whole aggregate of human life, physical, spiritual, intellectual and moral, individual, domestic and social, not with a view of reducing it in any way, but in order to elevate, regulate, perfect it, in accordance with the example and teaching of Christ." Particularly interesting to outsiders wishing to become better informed on the stand of the Church on the matter of separation of Church and State is a section dealing with the subject. Of pertinent interest, too, is the section on "The Subject of Education" with its examination of the philosophy of naturalism.

Fairchild, Hoxie Neale (editor). RELIGIOUS PERSPECTIVES IN COL-
LEGE TEACHING. New York: Ronald Press, 1952. Pp. x 460. 4.50

This volume brings together the essays published serially as pamphlets with the same title by the Edward W. Hazen Foundation. An introductory chapter presents the problems and principles, and the chapters which follow deal with religious perspectives in subjects such as English Literature, History, Philosophy, the Classics, Music, the Physical Sciences, Biology, Experimental Psychology, Sociology and Social Psychology, Anthropology, Economics, Political Science, and the preparation of teachers. The individual chapters were written by well-known scholars and teachers, and present what are probably the best stated objectives and perspectives of religion in higher education.

Ferré, Nels, Frederick S. CHRISTIAN FAITH AND HIGHER EDUCA-
TION. New York: Harper and Brothers, 1954. Pp. 251. 3.00

"Religion," in this book, is defined as "man's response as a whole to what he considers most important and most real." Co-relatively, "Education" is spoken of as "the assisting of seekers for more truth and a better life to appropriate for thmselves what is real, important, useful and satisfying." The book is intended to be a Christian philosophy of education. It reveals the author's broad and cultivated background in both philosophy and Religion, and makes use of the most recent writings and findings on the subject. Each of the chapters is interesting and significant, but among the more arresting for their views are: "What is Education?," "What is Religion?," "God as Educator," and "The University and the World."

FUNCTION OF THE PUBLIC SCHOOLS IN DEALING WITH
RELIGION, A Report on the Exploratory Study Made by the Com-
mittee on Religion and Education. Washington, D. C.: American
Council of Education, 1953. Pp. 145. 2.00

This small volume is the third of the reports published by the American Council on Education on the Appropriateness of Religion to Public Education in the U.S., with others released in 1944 and 1947. It purports to tell what the public schools, "in their own right and initiative, are doing to assist youth to have an intelligent understanding of the historical and contemporary role of religion in human affairs." Very informative are illustrations of current practices in schools and colleges, opinions of various leaders, the education of teachers and an 18-page Bibliography with brief annotations of each book.

Gaebelein, Frank Ely. CHRISTIAN EDUCATION IN A DEMOCRACY, The Report of the National Association of Evangelicals. New York: Oxford University Press, 1951. Pp. ix 305.   4.00

"While for evangelicals, historic Bible-centered Protestantism is the purest form of Christianity, in a democracy it does not enjoy a lot more privileges than Roman or Greek Catholicism, Mormonism, or Christian Science." With this statement as fundamental, the author develops a philosophy of Christian education intended to be workable for our age. The opening chapters analyze the contemporary scene, indicating how morality and religion have been bowed out of the classroom because it was considered undemocratic and authoritarian, and how secular naturalism has been allowed to take their place. The book abounds with quotable material showing how secularism has in the course of time filled in the vacuum produced by the enforcement of the principle of separation of church and state. Especially instructive chapters are entitled, "A New Form of American Education" dealing with the rise of Bible Colleges, "The Church as Educator," "Christian Education and the Home" and "The Unfinished Business of Christian Education."

Ginzberg, Eli. AGENDA FOR AMERICAN JEWS. New York: King's Crown Press, 1950. Pp. x 90.   2.00

Of especial interest for education and religion, in this volume, is Chapter IV, dealing with "Synagogue and School." Here, in definite and outlined form, the reader will find a review of the function of the Synagogue in Hebrew life. Out of the several paragraphs there emerges a view of the philosophy behind Jewish religion and education, and the problems faced by the relentless encroachment of secularism. The writer points out that Jewish education in the U.S., has been particularly handicapped by: (1) the fact that Hebrew schools have only recently come within the responsibility of the Synagogues; (2) a slow trend in religious education because of diligent care to avoid entanglements in ideological conflicts; and (3) the great need for voluntary contributions, in addition to the modest tuition, for supporting the religious program for children.

Hedley, George P. SUPERSTITIONS OF THE IRRELIGIOUS. New York: Macmillan Company, 1951. Pp. viii 140.   2.50

An answer to those who criticize religion and religious practices.

Superstitions about religion are defined and then the author, from his frame of reference, points out the fallacies of these superstitions.

Henry, Nelson B. (editor). MODERN PHILOSOPHIES AND EDUCATION, Part I, National Society for the Study of Education, 54th Yearbook. Chicago: Chicago University Press, 1955. Pp. 374. 4.00

To facilitate comparison of the different philosophies of education represented by the ten contributors to this volume, and also to avoid the confusion a massive text of this kind would present even to the intelligent reader, each writer was asked to address himself to six vital areas. Thus, each chapter is developed in terms of: (1) an opening section presenting the general philosophical orientation; (2) aims, values, and curriculum based on that orientation; (3) a development of the educative process, showing methods and motivations; (4) school and society; (5) the school and the individual; and (6) religious and moral education. In a separate chapter, then, each contributor proceeds to make clear a particular school of thought and its position on these matters. These views are developed: The Realistic View (John Wild) ; Thomist View (J. Maritain) ; Liberal Christian Idealism (T. Greene); Experimentalist View (G. R. Geiger) ; Marxist Philosophy of Education (R. S. Cohen); the Existentialist View (Ralph Harper) ; the Linguistic Approach (K. Burke) ; and the Ontological View (J. K. Feibleman). Though not intended as easy reading or as a brief summary of positions, the volume brings together for ready reference the diversities of philosophical schools as they bear on the subject of Education and religious values.

Henry, Virgil. THE PLACE OF RELIGION IN THE PUBLIC SCHOOLS, Handbook to Guide Communities. New York: Harper and Brothers, 1950. Pp. x 164. 2.50

The writer, the superintendent of schools in Orlando Park, Ill., says that the purpose of the book is to offer basic guidance to communities desiring to experiment with an objective study of religion in the public schools. The chapters of the book are organized so as to pursue suggestions for planning and operating a religious program. Thus, the first chapter has to do with "Realism in Planning" and this is followed by others on "Curriculum Proposals," "Selecting and Training Teachers," and "Expansion and Improvement with Experience." Of especial interest is the chapter on "Curriculum Proposals" and suggestions for studying Religion in Literature, Social Studies, the Physical and Biological Sciences, Music-Art-Drama, and in Assembly Programming. There is an extensive bibliography covering ten pages at the end of the book.

Hudson, Winthrop Still. THE GREAT TRADITION OF THE AMERICAN CHURCHES. New York: Harper and Brothers, 1953. Pp. 282. 3.75

"When churches succumb to the pressures of secular life and fail to exhibit a distinctive quality of faith and life, the separation of church and state with its clearly distinguished spheres of responsibility loses its point," says the author in his Foreword. And it is added that as the churches give less and less evidence of the prior claim of God upon their existence, the reason for their being independent of the state progressively diminishes. In the end, the churches find themselves with little to say that is not generally being said outside. "With the fading of a sense of distinctive vocation," he adds further, "church life inevitably begins to languish." The book examines the great and continuing tradition of the American churches of which Jonathan Edwards, Lyman Beecher, and Phillips Brooks have been outstanding representatives. Especially important is the undertone of thought that secular interference with the church is only possible because of grave weaknesses in the church and her sense of mission. "As the vigor and vitality of the churches decline, the pressure to call upon the state for help becomes almost irresistable . . ." Some very provocative chapters are titled, "An Axiom of All Americans: The Voluntary Prinicples in Religion," "Princes of the Pulpit: The Preachers and the New Theology," "The Church Embraces the World: Protestanism Succumbs to Complacency," and "The Renewal of the Churches: The Recovery of the Great Tradition."

Keller, James Gregory. ALL GOD'S CHILDREN, What Your Schools Can do For Them. New York: Hanover House Book, 1953. Pp. 292. 2.00

The moral earnestness of the book, its down-to-earth language and the positive theme that in Education as well as in everything else the American parent has a definite responsibility, has given this book wide circulation. Father Keller's theme is that there is something which each American can do to bring the knowledge of God back into Education. The language is very simple and the book itself is intended more for the parents and the general citizen than it is to serve as a textbook for classroom use.

Written by a Roman Catholic priest, the theme is non-sectarian and non-dogmatic in scope and treatment, and the material is presented from the standpoint of a man who feels it a matter of vital concern for religion to be felt in every phase of life. The book does not specify a program to be carried out in the classroom to teach Religion, but suggests ways in and out of the classroom for orienting thoughts and situations to the Divine Intelligence.

Kirsch, Felix M. THE RELIGIOUS TEACHER'S LIBRARY, A Selected Annotated List of Books, Pamphlets, and Magazines. Paterson, New Jersey: St. Anthony's Guild Press, 1940 (second edition, revised). Pp. vii 86. .50

Father Kirsch presents this descriptive list of books, pamphlets and magazines for the benefit of teachers of Religion, such as parents, priests, Brothers, Sisters, and lay catechists. It is a selective, annotated Bibliography of over 1,000 titles, each one with a brief description of what the reader may find in it. The material is divided into such subjects as "Teacher's Aids," "Textbooks," "Spiritual Reading,"

"Prayer Books," "Marriage and the Sex Problem," "Religious Plays," "Magazines," and a "Dictionary of Publishers."

Lowry, Howard. THE MIND'S ADVENTURE. Philadelphia: Westminster Press, 1950. Pp. 6-154. 2.50

Attempts to explain how higher education in this country became secular in nature. The place of religion in the college curriculum is discussed. A brief is made for the establishment of a department of religion in a liberal arts college program.

Madden, Ward Ellis. RELIGIOUS VALUES IN EDUCATION. New York: Harper and Brothers, 1951. Pp. xiii 203. 3.00

Madden proposes, in this text, to suggest how education can help in building a spiritual outlook adequate to the needs of the young people of our age. He uses "spiritual" not as the term is traditionally used, but in a more naturalistic and functional sense, as a quality operative in and extracted from, the highest ideals of the age in which we live. Hence, "The religious person . . . is the one who characteristically approaches life situations with an implicit faith that, no matter how good or bad these may be, something can be done to improve them. To be religious is to live with faith in the transformability of existence for the better." This, as against "the structured doctrinaire religions" is what Professor Madden urges for use in the public schools. Where "doctrinal or doctrinaire" religion would violate the principle of separation of Church and State, religious values based on experience is altogether justifiable. Much attention is given to value structure and the evolution of value consciousness, the discovery of social values through participation in "creative social activity," and to connecting a religious experience with artistic expression. The volume is seriously conceived, but is often over-synthetic, covering vast areas in limited compass. The viewpoint is naturalistic, and some chapters, especially those giving historical perspective, need to be watched for what are usually labelled "genetic fallacies."

Moberly, Walter Hamilton. THE CRISIS IN THE UNIVERSITY. New York: Macmillan Company, 1949. Pp. 316. 2.50

Chapter X of this volume, "Religion and Theology,"— Theology being defined as "the self-revelation of the living God, that is of a corporate experience of God in which, from start to finish He is the initiator"—will undoubtedly be of greatest interest for one concerned with the role of Religion in Education. The book as a whole examines the purpose of the university in the world of today, the nature of certain goals which were valid, and just when many English universities were first established but which have been rendered obsolete by the passage of time, and emphasizes a plea for Christian commitment in vital areas of thought. The final chapter, entitled "Taking Stock," contains the author's philosophy of education and recommendations for orienting the university to some ideals which are constant in the midst of change and also to an orientation which takes into account the recognition of newer purposes and ideals.

Murray, Albert Victor. EDUCATION INTO RELIGION. New York: Harper and Brothers, 1953. Pp. 230. 3.00

"Here are penetrating insights into the nature of religious experience, and the educational and theological foundations with which the religious educator must be concerned. In the background of the author's thought is the dilemma caught up in the very term, 'religious education' with its troublesome question: 'Can religion be *taught?*' Readers . . . will find especially interesting the implications for a philosophy of general education which seeks to find the proper relationship between religion and the public school. Dr. Murray is the president of Chestnut College, Cambridge, and writes from within the English setting of his problem . . . Some sections . . . of the presentation, such as the chapter on 'The Bible in Education' are directed to the teachers in the (English) day schools who are responsible for religious instruction. He emphasizes the distinctive task of the church, but finds wide opportunity for the school to teach the Bible and to discover its 'high correlation value' with such studies as geography, literature and history.

Education into Religion will have its greatest value, however, for those Christian educators who are seeking to develop a consistent philosophy of method in which sound educational procedures may be utilized in moving toward the goal of full fellowship within the historic Christian faith. The author indicates in his Preface that the title of the book contains his thesis: Christianity is an attitude to life *into* which the pupil has to grow. He then proceeds to attack the most difficult and basic problems of method.

Fundamental to the treatment of these problems is the analysis of the nature of Christian religion. Five elements are suggested: 'There is something to know, something to feel, something to choose, something to do, and something to belong to. Knowledge, feeling, morals, action, and belonging are all involved.' To meet these demands, Christian educators must properly relate their understanding of the stages of growth and the vital experiences of growing persons to their use of the great resources of the church: the Bible, Christian doctrine, and the worship and fellowship of the Christian community."

From the review of Frank W. Herriott in *Religious Education* XLIX, (July-August, 1954).

Neumann, Henry. LIVES IN THE MAKING, Aims and Ways of Character Education. New York: D. Appleton Company, 1932. Pp. xii 370. 3.00 (o.p.)

Newmann was at one time leader of the Brooklyn Society for Ethical Culture. His approach to the subject follows a pattern built upon an individual and community background. Virtues are tools for accomplishing personal and social ends. Many of the subjects of the author's concern have seen great advancement since 1932, but he has extensive material on the environment of the home, love-making and sex, community recreation and character through work, and the social spirit. The chapter on Religion cautions against allowing children to grow up without religion, accents toleration, and has much to say regarding touching the feelings and preparing the child for religious experience. Psychology, the Social and Natural Sciences, and Literature are dealt with from the standpoint of furthering ethical culture.

O'Leary, Mary Florence Margaret. THE CATHOLIC CHURCH AND EDUCATION. London: Burns, Oates and Washburne Ltd., 1943. Pp. x 118. 5s

"In order to understand the Christian concept of education, it is necessary in the first place to have a clear idea of man, his powers and destiny. It is also important to keep one's grasp upon the validity of objective truth." This sentence fairly well summarizes the intention of the volume. It represents a well thought out unfoldment of the Roman Catholic philosophy of Education. Often, the ideas contained therein elaborate the Encyclical of Pope Pius XI on the Christian Education of Youth. Chapter III, "The Struggle" examines the effect of current education on the child, the boy, the girl, the adult and the scholar, and contrasts it with Roman Catholic philosophy and ideals.

Ortega y Gasset, José. MISSION OF THE UNIVERSITY. Princeton: Princeton University Press, 1944. Pp. 103. 2.00 (o.p.)

"General education means the whole development of the individual, apart from his occupational training. It includes the civilizing of his life purpose, the refining of his emotional reactions, and the maturing of his understanding about the nature of things according to the best knowledge of our time." These sentences give the keynote of the author's philosophy. Moral and spiritual values are not taught deliberately so much as they are made part of the experience of life. What the University must be in addition to its normal curriculum of studies is taken up in the last chapter of this lecture to the Federation of University Students of Madrid.

Painter, Franklin, V. N. LUTHER ON EDUCATION, including a Historical Introduction and a Translation of the Reformer's Two Most Important Educational Treatises. Philadelphia: Lutheran Publication Society, 1889 (second edition). Pp. viii 281.

Painter's estimate is that Luther's "Letter to the Mayors and Aldermen of all the cities of Germany in behalf of Christian Schools" must be regarded as "the most important educational treatise ever written." The most elaborate of Luther's educational writings, "Sermon on the Duty of Sending Children to School," is translated and made a part of Luther's philosophy of education. Somewhat more than one-half of this book consists of the writer's Historical Introduction and a very clear picture of the state of education in Luther's time. Worth close reading are the chapters giving Luther's own comments on the state

19

of existing things. "The pitiable need that I recently witnessed, as visitor, has compelled me to prepare this catechism on Christian doctrine in such simple form. Alas! What a sad state of things I witnessed! The common people, especially in the villages, are utterly ignorant of the Christian doctrine; even many pastors are unqualified to teach; and yet all are called Christians, are baptized and partake of the sacrament, knowing neither the Lord's Prayer, the Creed, nor the Ten Commandments, and living and acting like irrational brutes!" There are many passages of overmastering eloquence.

Redden, John D., and Ryan, Francis A. FREEDOM THROUGH EDUCA-TION. Milwaukee: Bruce Publishing Company, 1944 Pp. xi 204. 2.50 (o.p.)

This volume presents an interpretation of the Four Freedoms—of Speech, Religion, from Want and from Fear—and how these can be made real and significant by education. The premise of the authors is that these freedoms have a moral foundation based on the truths of scholastic philosophy and divine revelation. The purpose of education is to assist man to achieve, in every way consistent with his rational nature, these needs: eternal life for his soul; truth about himself,—his world, his eternal destiny; goodness, whereby the will freely chooses to conform in conduct to eternal verities through love of God and man; and material well-being sufficient to enable him to realize and to promote his legitimate vocational ambition.

RELATION OF RELIGION TO PUBLIC EDUCATION; THE BASIC PRINCIPLES, by The Committee on Religion and Education of the American Council of Educational Studies. Washington, D. C.: American Council on Education, 1947. Pp. vii 54. 1.00

This is an excellent study of the background of present conditions, the basic philosophies in the social and intellectual life which gave rise to them, and the need for both understanding and a solution for present-day perplexities on the subject. Its view of the existing situation and the many difficulties on the subject raised by active opponents of the idea of Religious Education are made clear and fairly dealt with. There are pages of outstanding interest on "What we mean in Religion," "Shall the Schools Teach a Common Core of Religious Belief?," and "The Basic Responsibility of the Public Schools." The booklet seems to take especial pains to be positive at the same time that it avoids antagonizing.

Van Dusen, Henry Pitney. GOD IN EDUCATION, A Tract for the Times. New York: Charles Scribner's Sons, 1951. Pp. 9 128. 2.50

This essay grew out of a series of lectures on "Religion and Education" delivered at the University of Pittsburgh. It is valuable especially as showing the thought and insight of a prominent theologian and educator of what is lacking in Education at the present time. The writer's contention is that modern programs of Education reflect individualism, intellectualism, and dualization of truth and the universe which modern philosophy in general inherits from Descartes and other modern thinkers. The general thesis is that education cannot ignore Religion, and that without a religious foundation, knowledge has no place on which to throw an anchor.

Wilder, Amos N. (editor). LIBERAL LEARNING AND RELIGION: A Vital Discussion of major issues confronting the universities where there is Serious Concern for Religion. New York: Harper and Brothers, 1951. Pp. xi 338. 3.75

This volume is especially recommended for an overall view of the place of Religion in Education. The method of developing the material is to allow various well-known teachers, ministers, and college administrators to discuss the subject matter. There are such chapters as "Religious Faith and the Task of the Historian," "Liberal Learning and Religion in the American College," "The Teaching of Religion," "Academic Freedom," and "Psychotherapy, Religion and the Achievement of Selfhood." The chapters are easy to study, and authoritative without being scholarly and heavy.

Wilson, Karl K. HISTORICAL SURVEY OF RELIGIOUS CONTENT OF AMERICAN GEOGRAPHY TEXTBOOKS; from 1784 to 1895. A Doctoral Dissertation, University of Pittsburgh, 1951. Pp. 254.

Wilson's study shows that "There was a steady decline in the amount of space given to religious content as the principle of the separation of Church and State became more fully accepted by the people. History was often included in the early geography textbooks. The space allotted to each religion usually compared favorably to the number of its adherents." Quoted from Henry F. Spaulding, "Abstracts of Doctoral Dissertations in Religious Education, 1950-1, *Religious Education,* XLVII (1952, 208-31).

RELIGION IN THE HUMANITIES

A. PHILOSOPHY

Bennett, Charles Andrew A. **THE DILEMMA OF RELIGIOUS KNOWL-EDGE. New Haven: Yale University Press, 1931. Pp. xv 126. 2.00 (o.p.)**

The theme of these pages is primarily the problem of knowledge, and secondarily the problem and types of religious knowledge. The material included roams over the entire field of the philosophy of religion. Thus, Bennett discourses on the matters of immortality, the proofs of the existence of God, miracle, prophecy, prayer, revelation and the wrath of God. The chapters of the book were delivered as a lecture series in King's Chapel, Boston, in 1931. Bennett's thesis deftly fights against tendencies current in his and our time, to "humanize" religion and its tendency to have no God unless it be humanity itself. "His conviction is," says a classmate, William Ernest Hocking, "that all such naturalizings of religion denature it and lose its essence. They would turn religious language into metaphor, an analogy; they are thmselves mere analogies of religion." Again, "What Bennett puts into our hands . . . as a compass, is what I should call a doctrine or intuition; or, in his own language, an assertion of the kinship between religious and poetic inspiration." Some of the profound and subtle humor of the author may be evident in the insinuations of the last three chapters: "Naturalizing the Supernatural;" "Durkheim and the Sociological Humanists;" "Suffocation in the Subconscious: Freud and the Psychologists;" and "Metaphysical Respiration." There is this conclusion: "This fundamental need for a self-respect which rests upon self-knowledge is something which is frustrated by any subjectivist philosophy. Subjectivism forgets that man needs some Ultimate Other-than-Man against which he may measure himself; it fails to see that only the most outer can satisfy the most inner . . . The metaphysical pretensions of religion are the most important things about it."

Berkson, Issac Baer. **EDUCATION FACES THE FUTURE; An Appraisal of Contemporary Movements in Education. New York: Harper and Brothers, 1943. Pp. xii 345.   3.50**

Berkson's volume is concerned with educational philosophies, their premises, and the utilization of their ideas in curriculum construction and teaching methods. In Part I there is a succession of chapters grouped under the title of "Education and a Changing Liberal Philosophy," wherein "liberalism" is understood in a very broad sense as anti-traditional and as being, in general, the motive force behind change in all human institutions. In Part II there is a discussion of "Progressive Education in Transition," and the third part explains itself with the title, "School and Society in an Age of Reconstruction." Education is defined as "the art of bringing up children to live the good life in society," and each one of the essential terms of the definition is explained in the Summary chapter. There are several pages of selected references for reading. Some passing attention is given the role of Religion in Education, though the attitude toward Religion is strictly in keeping with the liberal and humanistic outlook.

Burtt, Edwin Arthur. TYPES OF RELIGIOUS PHILOSOPHY. New York: Harper and Brothers, 1951 (revised edition). Pp. xi 468. 4.50

This book intends to be an exposition of the main points of view in religious philosophies which now compete for acceptance among Western thinkers, together with an analysis of the major issues on which they differ. The volume should be serviceable to those who need or desire to know the philosophical content and the background of the various schools of religious thought which are active today. A Historical Setting provides a Hebrew Background, a Greek Background, and a brief history of the formation of orthodox theology. The major Western Philosophies of Religion which are considered and studied in detail, are the Catholic, Protestant Fundamentalism, the Religion of Science, Agnosticism, Ethical Idealism, Protestant Liberalism, Modernism and Humanism, and the New Supernaturalism. The implications of these for education are often brought out, and their major premises are scrutinized. Part III of the volume deals with disputed issues and those issues which bring misunderstanding and differences—man as a sinner, the role of faith, religion and social ethics, and others of the same nature. Appended to certain of the key chapters (as Catholicism, Protestant Fundamentalism, etc.) there are schematic tables presenting in outline, the major assumptions and views of man and his destiny of those schools.

Butler, James Donald. FOUR PHILOSOPHIES AND THEIR PRACTICE IN EDUCATION AND RELIGION. New York: Harper and Brothers, 1951. Pp. xiii 551. 4.50

Naturalism, Idealism, Realism, and Pragmatism, are the four philosophies examined in this volume, with their basic premises developed and made plain. As the latter part of the title indicates, each is tied in with Education and Religion. As philosophy texts are written, this is easier to read and to make use of. A detailed structural synopsis of what follows is presented at the beginning of each chapter, and the internal structure of each chapter is divided and captioned so that the development is easy to follow. Valuable for the student who wishes to pursue the subject further, is a long Bibliography at the end, broken down into primary and secondary source material. The concluding pages offer "A Confession of Faith: The Outline of a Philosophy."

Cabot, Richard Clarke. THE MEANING OF RIGHT AND WRONG. New York: Macmillan Company, 1933, Pp. x 463. 3.50 (o.p.)

Where the philosophy professor who writes a textbook on Ethics classifies and systematizes various theories of ethics, Cabot makes a living situation out of a problem and makes life and our next step depend upon it. Ethics, he says, rests on the study of consistency, growth, and self-deceit. Additional to his thesis are these ideas: (1) we are so made that according as we face or ignore facts we grow or degenerate; (2) persistency and stability and growth are the principles of right conduct. "Ethics is not the whole of a good life, nor even the best of it. In heroism, research, creative art and adoration, we forget ourselves. Unconscious of obligation we drive straight for the best in sight, by a path which I call by the unsatisfactory name of supermorality." The Table of Contents intrigued by its very structure: He considers certain principles of Right, gives them Application and Integration. Then he examines under Wrong, five familiar tricks of self-deceit. The Appendices consider "Some Unsolved Problems of Ethics," several Definitions basic in Ethics, and an analysis of the Declarations of War (1914-18) of 54 nations in terms of their ethical implications.

Conger, George Perrigo. THE IDEOLOGIES OF RELIGION. New York: Round Table Press, 1940. Pp. viii 271. 2.50

These "ideologies of religion" have risen to a place of prominence in our time primarily because Religion has been under severe attack. Hence the "ideologies" are nothing more than attempts to defend religion or to rescue it. They end either in rationalizing religion almost beyond recognition or by placing it altogether outside the range of human criticism or achievement. "To many men now, the older orthodoxies are stifling, the newer liberalisms superficial, and the newer supernaturalisms unreasonable." In the various chapters, Dr. Conger explains the nature and the weaknesses of Occultism, Mysticism, Supernaturalism, Idealism, Pragmatism, Evolutionism, Humanism, and Economic Nationalism. The final chapter, on "The Source and Object of Religion" seeks to be eclectic,—to keep the openness and range of Occultism, the sense of immediacy of Mysticism, and the Evolutionist's sense of process. The volume should be useful to those who find these ideas and ideals injected into education and the teaching processes.

Connell, Francis Jeremiah. OUTLINES OF MORAL THEOLOGY. Milwaukee: Bruce Publishing Company, 1953. Pp. 247. 3.75

In response to the increasing demand on the part of laymen for courses in Theology, this book attempts a presentation of the subject in terms as free from technicalities as it is possible. While the content of the book presumes a knowledge of or the acceptance of Roman Catholic teaching, much of the material can be studied in terms of its unfoldment from the principles which are initially laid down. There are separate chapters on such subjects as "The Final End of Man,"

"Conscience," "Sin," and "The Virtues in General." A second section of the book deals with the particular virtues: Faith, Hope, Charity, Justice, Prudence, Fortitude, and Temperance. Later chapters expound upon the Seven Sacraments of the Church.

Davidson, Robert Franklin. PHILOSOPHIES MEN LIVE BY. New York: Dial Press, 1952. Pp. vii 484. 5.00

An effort is made here, says the author, to make the insights of the great philosophers available to the beginner in terms he will understand, and in an appealing fashion. The intention, of the book, is to relate the study of philosophy to the moral and religious problems of the student. Some fifteen or sixteen philosophers are dealt with, and their thought used as the solution to the specific problems with which they were concerned. There is a section on "The Pursuit of Pleasure," wherein Hedonism and Utilitarianism are examined. A second section deals with "The Life of Reason" and examines the rationalism of The Stoics, of Spinoza, and the modern expression of it in Walter Lippman. In the third section, the Naturalism of Nietzsche, the Pragmatism of James, and Dewey's Naturalistic Humanism are passed in review. Finally there is an examination of "The Compulsion of the Idea," which involves the Idealism of Plato and Aristotle, Kant's Moral Imperative, and Niebuhr's Christian Idealism. In the end, the author offers "A Philosophy for These Times," in which he seeks to effect a synthesis of the best elements in the philosophies examined. There is appended a very long list of Suggested Readings which should be of service.

Dewey, John. A COMMON FAITH. New Haven: Yale University Press, 1934. Pp. 87. 2.75

In these Terry Lectures, the eminent representative of the naturalistic attitude on life and its social institutions, examines the claims of supernatural religion and religion as a personal experience. He argues for concreteness and definiteness, but he is not iconoclastic. He respects the traditions of civilization and of a humanity which has interacted with nature to bring them forth. But "Ours is the responsibility of conserving, transmitting, rectifying and expanding the heritage of values we have received, that those who come after us may receive it more solid and secure . . . Here are all the elements for a religious faith that shall not be confined to sect, class, or race. Such a faith has always been implicitly the faith of mankind. It remains to make it explicit and militant."

Everett, Millard Spencer. IDEALS OF LIFE; An Introduction to Ethics and the Humanities: With Readings. New York: John Wiley and Sons, Inc., 1954. Pp. 736. 5.00

A vast variety of subjects are covered in this book, as the extensive Index shows, from anti-Semitism to missionary Zeal. In fact, Prof. Everett seems to have taken the world for his subject and related all things to Ethics and the Humanities. Appended to the text there are also some 30 pages of questions for discussion. The volume is divided into seven parts, and deals successively with Ideals of Life, Moral Fixation, Liberal Morality, Personal and Family Morality, the Ethics of Democracy, Moral Training and Moral Theory, and the Liberal Philosophy of History. The outlook of the writer is humanistic, and he has much to say about Education and Religion as they fit into a humanistic framework. His political outlook favors a Democracy, and the text is so oriented that it is intended to be serviceable to students in a democratic society. As the sub-title indicates, Everett writes a book for use in courses in the humanities as well as for the narrower concern of philosophical Ethics.

Hartshorne, Charles, and Reese, William L. PHILOSOPHERS SPEAK OF GOD. Chicago: University of Chicago Press, 1953. Pp. 535. 7.50

"This work aims to present—by selections from some fifty writers ranging from Lao-tse, Plato and Shankara to Whitehead, Berdyaev, and Radhakrishnan—the chief philosophical conceptions of deity. It also aims to aid readers in estimating the validity of these conceptions. The work is thus two things: (1) a book of readings in philosophical theology—the first of its kind— and (2) a systematic analysis and evaluation of theistic (and atheistic) ideas." Such is the plan of the writers as they explain it in the Preface. It is explained that this is not an anthology of religious writings; rather it is a philosophical treatment of central religious ideas. The selections are arranged according to Classical Views, Modern Views, and Skeptical or Atheistic Views—Ancient and Modern. Each of those is subdivided into five or six further parts, and the selections arranged accordingly. In the Introduction and more especially in the Epilogue, the authors qualify their particular outlook, termed "Panentheism." The term is explained thus: "Panentheism holds that we are accidents in God, and thus it is equally opposed to the classical (theism) . . . and the pantheistic (conceptions) . . . Or, in other terms, panentheism conceives process, becoming, as real in God; classical theism as real outside God, and pantheism as somehow unreal but insofar as real, in God." (p. 163a). The lengthy Index shows the wide range of history from which the authors have drawn their material.

Huxley, Aldous Leonard. THE PERENNIAL PHILOSOPHY. New York: Harper and Brothers, 1945. Pp. xi 312. 4.00

The Perennial Philosophy is both the title of the book and the Divine Reality which is at the foundation of all things. In this volume Huxley elucidates both by commentary and quotation the Eternal Truth of which the religious philosophers have left record. Needless to say, the entire emphasis of the book is on the common bond which links together philosophers both of the East and of the West. Especially full chapters are those which deal with "God in the World," "That art Thou," "Truth," "Self-Knowledge," "Time and Free Will," "Ritual, Symbol and Sacrament," and "Contemplation, Action, and Social Utility."

26

Hyde, William DeWitt. THE FIVE GREAT PHILOSOPHIES OF LIFE.
New York: Macmillan Company, 1928. Pp. x 296. 3.75

Some of the higher elements of personality rise above the threshold
of consciousness, are reducible to principles, and are amendable to
rational control. Thus they can be consciously employed to shape the
direction of our life. President Hyde (of Bowdoin College) holds
that the five centuries from the birth of Socrates to the death of Christ
produced five schools of thought each of which represents a guiding
principle of human personality. These are: the Epicurean pursuit of
pleasure, genial, but ungenerous; the Stoic law of self-control, strenu-
ous but forbidding; the Platonic plan of subordination, sublime but
ascetic; the Aristotelian sense of proportion, practical, but uninspiring; and the Christian Spirit of Love, broadest and deepest of these.
The plan of the book, he says, is to let the masters of these principles
of personality speak in their own words. The author provides sufficient running commentary to clarify words requiring clarification.

Kallen, Horace Meyer. THE EDUCATION OF FREE MEN; An Essay
toward a Philosophy of Education for Americans. New York: Farrar,
Straus and Company, 1949. Pp. xix 332. 5.00

"A philosophy of education but focuses philosophic appraisal on the
sciences and arts of communication as these are involved in teaching
and learning. It inquires into the goods of life that men strive to attain, the evils they labor to avoid or overcome . . ." The writer so
heralds his theme. And he adds that the task of education, in each
culture, is to realize the ideal of manhood it cherishes; in our place
and time, our faith is in the ideal of the Free Man. The Free Man is
the man whose life conforms to "the laws of nature and of Nature's
God." There is an analysis of the school as an institution, of the democratic temper and its educational enterprise, of social organization and
personal liberty, and finally, the life and labor of free men. In one of
the chapters—"Personality and the Religious Interest"—attention is
given to the philosophics underlying various religious groups, religious authoritarianism and constitutional guarantees. Though the author's outlook is reflected on every page, his "liberalism" is best
reviewed in the last chapter, "The Liberal Education of the Modern
Man."

Robinson, Daniel Sommer. THE PRINCIPLES OF CONDUCT, An Introduction to Theoretical and Applied Ethics. New York: Appleton-
Century Crofts, Inc., 1948. Pp. xviii 420. 3.25

Though intended primarily as a textbook for beginners in Ethics,
this volume is written so as to be helpful to the general reader as well.
It describes and appraises the theories of the various ethical schools,
the general principles of ethics and their application, and purposes to
help students to formulate a sound philosophy of life. Because the
writer is convinced that the exploitation of atomic energy marks the
beginning of a new era in human affairs, he devotes three chapters to
ethics as seen through this new perspective.

The outlook of the writer may be described as broad and eclectic. His descriptions of the genetic, comparative, statistical, historical, psychological, theological, and intuitive methods which form the foundations of the various ethical schools are fair and adequate within the limited compass set by the book.

Especially noteworthy are the chapters on ethics for an atomic age, one on the moral teachings of the great sages, and another on Rights, Duties, and Justice. Of practical interest are the additional sections on Ethics related to the democratic form of government, Ethics in Education, and theoretical codes of the professions and businesses.

Sayers, Ephraim Vern. THE FIRST COURSE IN PHILOSOPHY OF EDU-
CATION; A Syllabus and Source Book. New York: Henry Holt and
Company, 1952. Pp. xv 399. 3.90

In this volume, the various schools of philosophy are found at the heart of social and educational situations. To untangle the situation enables the individual to discover the thought motivation which brought it about. The author says that such is his deliberate method of introducing the student to a Philosophy of Education: "The theory of the book is that, if we . . . keep ourselves at the task of clearing up differences in our social perspectives . . . we shall eventually move full force into the areas . . . where philosophers fall out most violently." There is an especially meaningful section (Part III) on "Contrasting Conceptions of the Nature of Man," and another (Part IV) on "Viewpoints on the Improvement of Life." In this latter there are perspectives on "The Good," "The Right," "Science and Morals," and "The Religious Attitude." At the end there is a long booklist (17 pp.) with helpful suggestions for further readings.

Spann, John Richard (editor). THE CHURCH AND SOCIAL RESPONSI-
BILITY. Nashville: Abingdon-Cokesbury Press, 1953. Pp. 272. 2.75

As a symposium, the intent of the various writers seems to be to answer the perennial question, "What then shall we do?" As against one extreme which holds that man can do nothing, God everything, and the church has no social responsibility, there is the other holding that the entire burden, is on man, that without him God can do nothing and the main task of the church is to promote social progress.

"The writers of this symposium avoid the extreme, but their leanings are definitely toward the activist and away from the quietistic approach. The book will be enjoyed by the social actionists who in late years have felt the tide of social thought running against them . . . It will also prove a wholesome corrective for the thinking of some of our younger ministers whose theological education has been dominated by Barthian schools of thought. Religious educators will here find much to corroborate one of the basic assumptions of modern education—that nothing is learned until it is put into practice."

From the review by Victor H. Keiser, *Religious Education,* XLIX (May-June, 1954). It is to be gathered that Part I deals with the basic theological grounds for the social ministry of the church. Part II is on Basic Human Rights and the Community, Part III has to do with "The Church and the Economic Order," and Part IV with "The Church and the Political Order." There are outstandingly interesting essays with these titles: "Daily Work and Christian Vocation," by Cameron Hall; "The Organization of Economic Life," by Walter G. Muelder; "The Christian Citizen," by Robert Fitch; "The Church in the Prevention and Treatment of Crime," by Harold de Wulf; and "War and the Christian Ethic," by Ronald H. Bainton. "In all these chapters there is the clear recognition that while the church and the state must not be made subservient either to the other, yet because each deals with the same people for purposes which are not identical, but complementary, they must work as partners."

Stace, Walter Terence. THE CONCEPT OF MORALS. New York: Macmillan Company, 1937. Pp. xi 307. 2.25 (o.p.)

Stace says very openly and forthrightly that his sympathy lies with the tendency to regard ethics and morals as *relative* to their circumstances, the time and place of their appearance as well as to the natures of men. Yet, he sets himself squarely against the tendency to carry this relativistic ethics to complete *subjectivity*. "If there is no kind of standard to which the music of Beethoven can be judged superior to any barbarian's tom-tom, then what is the sense of aesthetic education? Why trouble to teach our children what we believe to be great art . . .?" The volume is a fine commentary on the extremes to which certain philosophical notions can be carried, and the author writes very lucidly. He seeks to avoid the "left wing" philosophical group and the "right wing" philosophical group, and keep morals and beauty and truth within the framework of a particular culture. "Our civilization is a Christian civilization. It has grown up during nearly two thousand years upon the soil of Christian monotheism. In this soil our whole outlook upon life and consequently all our moral ideas, have their roots." Interesting chapters deal with such subjects as "Ethical Relativity," "The Unity of Morals," "The University of Morals," and "Why Should I be Moral?"

Wieman, Henry Nelson, and Meland, Bernard E. AMERICAN PHILOSOPHIES OF RELIGION. New York: Harper and Brothers, 1936. Pp. xiii 370. 3.00 (o.p.)

Varied views of contemporary types of thought in American philosophy of religion are gathered together here. The authors say that their objective is to clarify the current confusion in modern thought by providing a perspective to view the present scene. Among its merits, the book groups together the different philosophies in terms of their relationship with each other and in terms of common origin. Actually, these American philosophies are considered as offshoots of four basic patterns: those rooted in Supernaturalism; those rooted in Idealism; those rooted in Romanticism; and those rooted in Naturalism and the Scientific Method. Within these divisions there are still further subdivisions. Each particular chapter gives a brief summary, often with selected quotations, of American philosophers sharing a religious outlook, though that outlook varies from a supernatural assumption to that of the modern scientific "liberal." At the end there is a Symposium with brief essays by well-known scholars who are representatives of the type of religion considered in the text, and the essays are grouped under the title "The Present Outlook in Philosophy of Religion."

B. PSYCHOLOGY

Adler, Alfred. UNDERSTANDING HUMAN NATURE. New York: Greenberg, Publisher, Inc., 1927. Pp. xiii 286. 3.50

Understanding Human Nature is a summary of a series of lectures representing the fundamentals of Individual Psychology,—Adler's own school of thought. The application of the principles of individual psychology to everyday conduct, the organization of the personal life, and how lack of harmony in individual behavior affects the harmony of social life, are the basic themes of the book. The helpfulness of this volume lies in its connecting Psychology with character education on the one hand, and Religion to a humanistic philosophy of life on the other. There is a fine analysis of the psyche and its functions and faculties. Part III deals with "The Science of Character."

Allan, Denison Maurice. THE REALM OF PERSONALITY. Nashville: Abingdon-Cokesbury Press, 1947. Pp. 249. 3.00

Allan, in this volume, brings together those teachings of modern Psychology and Philosophy which can be fruitfully related to the truths of Christianity. In his Foreword he says that three convictions find verification from the contemporary scene. "The first is that the very variety of the psychological schools bears testimony to the inherent richness of human individuality . . . The second is that the philosophic framework known as the 'doctrine of levels' and subscribed to in some form by almost all of the great philosophers offers the most fruitful synthesis of the facts of Psychology and the truths of Christianity . . . The third conviction is that, clearly understood the contemporary emphasis on the integrative power of the brain and the Christian teaching as to the immortality of the person, offer no contradiction to each other." Especially helpful for study and thought is the first chapter on "The Rival Views of Personality," where the Naturalistic, Humanistic and Transcendental Views of Man are contrasted and compared. The thoughts of the writer are eloquent testimony to the influence of the teachers to whom he acknowledges debt: William McDougall, William E. Hocking, Ralph B. Perry, and Alfred North Whitehead.

Allport, Gordon W. THE INDIVIDUAL AND HIS RELIGION. New York: Macmillan Company, 1953. Pp. xi 147. 2.50

What is the place of religion in the life economy of the individual?

Allport sets himself the task of discovering, in part, the answer to this question. The author discusses such things as these: Religion in childhood; Conscience and Conflict; Organic desire as a basis of religious sentiment; The nature of Doubt; The Origins of the religious quest; Individual validation of faith; Intention; Maturity in religion; Prayer; Sentiment; Validation of Faith; Value; and the Religion of Youth.

A constant thesis of the publication is the seeking of the role of religion within personality structure.

Allport, Gordon, W. BECOMING; Basic Considerations for a Psychology of Personality. New Haven: Yale University Press, 1955. Pp. ix 106. 2.75

The reader probably could be best oriented to this book by reading Chapter 10, "Is the Concept of Self Necessary?" For it is necessary for the reader to have an understanding of the concept of self before the rest of the chapters of this publication fall into place. A background knowledge of psychology and philosophy will help the reader obtain the full value of *Becoming*. Allport's references range over a wide area. The reader is introduced to the ideas of many individuals such as these: Sigmund Freud, Erich Fromm, Carl Rogers, Kurt Goldstein, Joseph Wood Krutch, Paul Tillich, and Edmund Sinnott. The reader further becomes cognizant of terms such as these: ego, empiricism, existentialism, hedonism, homeostasis, proprium, and self. It can be seen that this book contains many excellent facets which a reader may pursue in securing a greater knowledge of the development of the self. Section 21 discusses "Religious Sentiment."

Dreikurs, Rudolph. CHARACTER EDUCATION AND SPIRITUAL VALUES IN AN ANXIOUS AGE. Boston: Beacon Press, 1954. Pp. 23. .50

Dreikurs is professor of Psychiatry at the Chicago Medical School, and this pamphlet is a reprint of the address delivered at the 125th Anniversary meeting of the Unitarian Sunday School Society. The writer calls for a re-examination of the "traditional" and "authoritarian" ways of teaching children, stressing that the reason why youth is in revolt against its elders is because of attempts to compel obedience rather than co-operation. "We no longer believe," he says, "in the inborn goodness or badness of individuals . . . there are no 'bad' children only unhappy ones who have not found the proper approach to the social problems confronting them."

Fromm, Erich. MAN FOR HIMSELF; An Inquiry into the Psychology of Ethics. New York: Rinehart and Company, Inc., 1947. Pp. xiv 254. 3.75

This well-known student of Freud and "neo-Freudian" in the sense that he modifies the ideas of Freud for adaptation to modern conditions, undertakes in this book "to discuss the problems of ethics and norms of value leading to the realization of man's self and of his potentialities. It continues the ideas expressed in the previous *ESCAPE FROM FREEDOM*. The author says that his experience as a phychologist has convinced him that the problem of ethics cannot be omitted from the study of personality, either theoretically or therapeutically. The writer, to avoid relativism with its abandonment of objectively valid norms of conduct on one hand and authoritarianism, with what is called its frequent irrationality, adopts as his view "humanistic ethics," "—the idea that only man (not a transcedent Being) determines the critera for virtue and sin. "Good" is what is good for man; "evil" is what is detrimental. The sole criterion is his welfare. Of especial interest, in this light, are the chapters on Personality and its Integration, and the Problems of Humanistic Ethics as these have a bearing on the integration of character.

Hollingworth, Harry L. PSYCHOLOGY AND ETHICS; A Study of The Sense of Obligation. New York: Ronald Press Company, 1949. Pp. ix 247. 4.00

To take the subject of ethics out of the clouds and to give it a solid anchorage in the psychology of everyday life, Dr. Hollingworth says is the aim of this study. He would place the study of moral conduct on a scientific and measurable basis. "Traditional systems of ethical doctrine," he observes, "do not relate very closely to contemporary activities and ideals, and they are often based on antiquated descriptions of our minds and misguided accounts of human motives." Conscience and traditional indoctrination seem to be identified together, and the sense of the "ought" and emulation of examples set down in early training seem to be used synonymously. The resultant conduct is then described with scientific objectivity rather than condemned or decried. The writer says that the book should prove useful in courses in education, social psychology, human relations, and ethics. Of especial interest is an "Ethical Insight Test," "A Tentative Outline for a Course on the Meaning of Ought," and a chapter on "Ethics and the Schools of Psychology."

James, William. TALKS TO TEACHERS ON PSYCHOLOGY: And to Students on Some of Life's Ideals. New York: Henry Holt and Company, 1914. unpaged 2.00 (o.p.)

"My main desire," says the author in presenting this greatly simplified account of Psychology and its work, "has been to make them (teachers) conceive, and if possible, reproduce sympathetically in their imagination, the mental life of their pupils as a sort of active unity which he himself feels it to be." In the text, the subject is made alive, and such things as behavior, consciousness, habit, interest and the like, are never separated from the conception of the wholeness of life. In the chapter on "Education and Behavior" education is defined as "the organization of acquired habits of conduct and tendencies to behavior," and thus the link between education and conduct is established. The teacher's art consists largely in substituting higher for lower reactions. The chapter on "The Laws of Habit" is very lucid and inspiring. There are three talks to students that show James as both a psychologist and philosopher: "The Gospel of Relaxation," "On a Certain Blindness in Human Beings," and "What makes a Life Significant?"

Jung, Carl Gustav. MODERN MAN IN SEARCH OF A SOUL. New York: Harcourt Brace and Company, 1933. Pp. ix 282. 5.00

As the translator tells us, in this volume Dr. Jung speaks in convincing terms to those who believe that if they can attain more knowledge of the innerworkings of their own minds, and more information of the less definite laws which govern the psyche, they can achieve the new attitude that is demanded without either regressing to a mediaeval theology on the one hand, or becoming victims to the illusions of 19th century ideology on the other.

Though written for the ordinary reader and generally free from the frequent obscurities which characterize his works, the student will find easiest to understand and most pertinent to the connection between Religion and Psychology, the last two chapters. These bear the titles, "The Spiritual Problems of Modern Man" and "Psychotherapists or the Clergy."

King, William Peter (editor). BEHAVIORISM; A BATTLE LINE. Nashville, Tenn.: The Cokesbury Press, 1930. Pp. 5 376. 2.25

This series of essays by prominent psychologists, clergymen and educators is distinguished by the fact that all of the contributors take a common stand in opposition to materialistic Behaviorism. Behaviorism, once labelled also "somatology," says Dr. Morse in the Introduction, is a natural offshoot of materialistic antomology and cosmology and atheistic theology. As such it is not new, and is to be found in different historical periods. Here the individual under attack is John B. Watson, the "father" of modern psychological Behaviorism. And Watson defines his platform thus: "The rule, or measuring rod, which the behaviorist puts in front of him always is: 'Can I describe this bit of behavior in terms of "stimulus and response"?' The text is organized on the basis of a triple division: "The General Principles of Behaviorism," "Behaviorism and Value," and "Behaviorism and Metaphysics." Prof. William McDougall, Dr. Edgar S. Brightman, Dr. Rufus Jones and Bishop Francis J. McConnell are among the contributors—of whom there are twenty-seven in all. A Jewish Rabbi contributes a chapter on "Behaviorism and Religion," a philosopher contributes "Can a Behaviorist be Good?," and Dr. Jones writes a chapter on "Have Souls Gone out of Fashion?" At the end of the book there is a useful selected bibliography.

Ligon, Ernest Mayfield. A GREATER GENERATION. New York: Macmillan Company, 1948. Pp. xii 157. 2.75

"It is a firm conviction of the author that the laws of character development are as definite a part of the very nature of things as the laws of the physical universe. Therefore they are to be discovered by research, not invented by personal opinion." For the information of parents, teachers of youth, ministers and students, this little volume was organized to describe the methods and principles of the character education which has been developed in the Union College Character Research Project (Schenectady, N. Y.)

The Project, carried on in the department of Psychology, takes advantage of the effectiveness of the scientific method, and applies it to increase character education. A basic starting point is that "in teaching children, the laws of learning must be obeyed if they are to learn;" the child must be converted from a hearer to a doer of the word. Chapter XII, "The Christian Hypothesis" is rooted in the Beatitudes of the Sermon on the Mount. In general, Part II of the book, "The Role of Religion in the Problem of Character" may prove most interesting, but the entire volume is simply written and reduces character education to workable details.

Link, Henry Charles. THE RETURN TO RELIGION. New York: Macmillan Company, 1936. Pp. 181. 2.50

In these pages which are partly autobiographical and partly in the nature of an essay on the subject, an eminent American psychologist describes the elements of a liberal arts education which estranged him from religion and the experiences of life which were responsible for his return to religion. There is much material for serious reflection pertinent to the content of formal education and also to formal religion. He brings out the weaknesses of many shibboleths of psychology and also the good sense which the trials of life can restore to the man who has never valued it. Some chapters are entitled: "The Achievement of Happiness," "Fools of Reason" (neuroses of the educated), "Wine at Weddings" (including Religious Conflicts), "Love and Marriage," and "The Vice of Education."

McDougall, William. CHARACTER AND THE CONDUCT OF LIFE; Practical Psychology for Everyman. New York: G. P. Putnam's Sons, 1927. Pp. xiv 394. 5.00 (o.p.)

It may be said that the spirit of this volume is reflected in the sentence from Edmund Burke quoted on its title page: "It is the prerogative of man to be in a great degree a creature of his own making." While Professor McDougall makes a deliberate attempt to steer clear of Religion in this volume, the material of the book has for its clear purpose the development of character by reflection of the powers which man has at his command. There are chapters on "Our Need of Criticism," "Modifications of Original Disposition," "Character and Will," "Habits and Principles," and an examination of "Some Common Faults." In the Appendix there is a helpful and informative section on "Management of the Body."

McDougall, William. THE FRONTIERS OF PSYCHOLOGY. New York: D. Appleton-Century Company, Inc., 1934. Pp. xi 235. 2.00 (o.p.)

Specialization, in any of the studies in which man engages, brings the danger of narrowness and identification with a limited school of thought. From that danger, Psychology is no more exempt than any other study, and the broad understanding of McDougall gives a refreshing interest to this subject. By "Frontiers" is meant those outposts where Psychology ceases to be merely Psychology and touches on Philosophy, Science, History, Mental and Moral Evolution and related subjects. While no discussion of Education and Religion is involved in a direct way, much is said about the nature of value, the direction of human evolution, and belief in the self. "We may sum up," says the author, "by saying that all the Twentieth Century sciences of life are pointing us away from the rationalistic mechanistic theory of man, which Nietzche called the Apollonian theory, and back to age-long rival, the Dionysian theory."

May, Rollo. MAN'S SEARCH FOR HIMSELF. New York: W. W. Norton and Company, 1952. Pp. 281. 3.50

This book of applied psychology is written in an effort to help the individual come to grips in a personal way with his own problems. The writer charts a course by which individuals can face insecurity. The book should be very popular with college students or others seeking ways and means of solving their own conflicts.

Scheidlinger, Saul. PSYCHOANALYSIS AND GROUP BEHAVIOR; A Study of Freudian Group Psychology. New York: W. W. Norton and Company, 1952. Pp. xviii 245. 3.75

"This is an exceedingly important book for students of group dynamics. The first half . . . contains an excellent summary of Freudian theory of personality development, and an analysis of Freud's teaching about basic group processes and the role of a group leader. The second half is devoted to an equally excellent analysis of the implications and applications of the Freudian theory, including a good critique of sociometry and field theory psychology, as well as a chapter on the implications for education . . .

"The teacher or the group worker will find here many fruitful insights and will be stimulated to look more carefully at the behavior of the groups he is working with. I would make this required reading for the advanced student in religious education. One additional value of this book is that it contains an extensive bibliography on the subject." From the review by Paul B. Maves, *Religious Education*, XLIX (July-August, 1954).

C. THE STUDY OF LITERATURE

Baldwin, Robert Chester, and McPeek, James A. S. AN INTRODUCTION TO PHILOSOPHY THROUGH LITERATURE. New York: Ronald Press Company, 1950. Pp. xxi 595. (o.p.)

The writers say that the purpose of this book is to introduce students to philosophy through the medium of selections from good literature. There are selections from more than one-hundred authors, for the most part contemporary writers, and the basis for the reading selections was clarity, vividness, and effectiveness of expression. The material, in general, could be employed to introduce students to Philosophy through Literature or to Literature through readings of philosophic import. An opening chapter deals with "The Great Questions," of the Meaning of Life, and others have to do with "Of Human Conduct," "In Search of God," "If a Man Die," "The Problem of Evil," "The Value of Life—both Humanist and Naturalist," and "Some Aspects of Pragmatism." The authors vouch for the effectiveness of the text in achieving its purpose, and the reader will find the selections very provocative to the student mind.

Demiashkevich, Michael John. THE NATIONAL MIND, English-French-German. New York: American Book Company, 1938. Pp. xii 508. 3.50 (o.p.)

This study is greatly to be valued because the literature of the peoples mentioned is used as a looking glass to mirror their life and culture and ideals. Literature reflects character, and character reveals, either consciously or unconsciously, religion, education, and life's goals. The study of the English Mind, thus, shows us the Englishman as a solid citizen, his tenacity of purpose, his political mystism, and the ideals of the gentleman, of fair play, and what is often a narrow double standard of judgment. Much of representative English literature shows us the characteristic conservatism, emotional control, the art of compromise, and the acceptance of the hierarchical principle. The author illustrates these traits with situations taken from English writers. The same service is rendered the French mind,—out of French literature discovering conscious and unconscious revelations of rationalism, expression, sociability, easy captivity by the witchery of formulas, and political mysticism. The German novel and drama, likewise, reveal what Prof. Demiashkevich calls "The basic discord of the German mind," its "Dionysian fraternization with nature," its aspirations toward "totalitarianism," and its aspirations after a mystical, but political "unity." The work is amply illustrated with examples taken from literary works, political situations, and episodes reflecting the basic national character.

Jones, Howard Mumford. IDEAS IN AMERICA. Cambridge, Mass.: Harvard University Press, 1944. Pp. xi 304. 3.00

"If the United States has not developed a Shakespeare or a Milton, Great Britain has not developed a Whitman or a Mark Twain . . . hence one of the several justifications for the study of American "literary history." For it is one of the contentions of the author that even as Shakespeare and Milton reveal certain ruling ideas of life, so do the American writers who should be understood in that context. Dean Jones says "How long can we safely permit our students to believe that the rise of industry is all there is to the study of American life? . . . The spirit of Emerson is likewise American. We have neglected the resources of our spiritual life too long—I trust that we shall not have to pay dearly for our neglect in the materialism of which so many now complain, or in a narrow and extravagant nationalism, which, uncorrected by an understanding, not only of the spiritual struggle of mankind at large, but also of an understanding of the larger purposes of life in this republic, may yet obliterate the America of Emerson in the America of Ford." The 65 pages or so of notes at the end of the text form a rich commentary on the sources for his study employed by the author.

Jones, Howard Mumford. THE THEORY OF AMERICAN LITERATURE. Ithaca, New York: Cornell University Press, 1948. Pp. ix 208. 2.75

Dean Jones classifies this work as "literary history," and in any analysis of a national literature, a writer cannot avoid delving into the ideas, philosophical and religious, which form the background of that literature. That moral and spiritual values cannot be avoided is evident in the obvious philosophical and at times religious implications of the chapter headings: "The Literary Spirit of Each Age," "Where Liberty Exalts the Mind," and "A National Spirit in Letters." In its original form, this book consisted of six lectures delivered at Cornell University as the Messenger Lectures on the "Evolution of Civilization." In the main, this work not only surveys the letters and books which form the record of American life, but has occasional commentaries on such philosophies as have from time to time invaded America and have left their mark in literary periods, as Idealism, Humanism, Freudianism, and others less known. A serviceable guide for the student is found in the appendix, which has a list arranged chronologically, of "Works on the History and Philosophy of American Literature."

Miller, Perry Gilbert E. THE NEW ENGLAND MIND; The Seventeenth Century. Cambridge, Mass.: Harvard University Press, 1954. Pp. xi 528. 6.50

Miller stated that in this book he has taken the liberty of treating the whole literature as though it were the product of a single intelligence, a "Puritan mind," as it were. And for all practical purposes the literature of the period was a reflection, mirrored large, of a Calvinistic theology and outlook on life which left its mark on all human effort. "Regardless of the repute in which it may be held today, Puritanism is of immense historical importance: it was not only the most coherent and most powerful single factor in the early history of America, it was a vital expression of a crucial period in European development . . ."The four books composing the volume are divided into "Religion and Learning," "Cosmology," "Anthropology," and "Sociology." The religion begins in the theology of St. Augustine and culminates in the piety which was a feature of early Puritan morality. The Sociology is actually a social covenant, which the writers of the period understood as binding a people in New England to God with the same cords as he bound his chosen people in the Old Testament. Prof. Miller's volume is very scholarly and abounds with factual material. The very profuse notes at the end not only give a proper idea of the sources consulted, but expand the horizon for further study.

Scheele, Sister M. Augustine. EDUCATIONAL ASPECTS OF SPIRITUAL WRITINGS. Milwaukee: St. Joseph Press, 1940. Pp. xiii 273.

In this published dissertation, previously submitted as part of the requirement for the Ph.D. degree, the writer attempts to show how the literature of spirituality may be used to shape the moral and spiritual character of youth. The author says that in the spiritual foundations of man alone, is there any possibility of fortifying youth against the materialism of the day. Three of the historically outstanding classics of the inner-life are included in this study: The *Confessions* of St. Augustine; Gerard Groote's *The Following of Christ* (the prototype of a Kempis' *The Imitation of Christ*) and the *Spiritual Exercises* of St. Ignatius de Loyola. In three chapters, the books are analyzed and their method of spiritual development described. In the final chapter, the author draws together into a fine synthesis the "Contributions of Spiritual Writings to Contemporary Educational Thought." Highly valuable and useful is the bibliography at the end. It has annotations of varying length about the books listed. These cover some 30 pages.

Weatherhead, Leslie Dixon. PSYCHOLOGY IN THE SERVICE OF SOUL. London: Epworth Press, 1951 (21st Impression). Pp. xiii 226.

Dr. Weatherhead, a Methodist minister, with a very large following in London, has carried on extensive studies in Psychology in addition to his training and duties as a minister, and in this volume Religion and Psychology are made serviceable to each other. He says that his purpose in the book includes showing distressed men and women that there is a path through the dark wood and they can be helped to find it; suggesting to young ministers who are willing to work hard that by becoming true, efficient, and understanding physicians of souls, they can do a work which the Master of Life needs doing; to suggest to the reader that Freudian methods can be applied without accepting Freud's philosophy, and that the aim of practical psychology is that of the New Testament—namely, the facing up to life bravely, and the making of it that vigorous, radiant, confident, healthful thing God meant it to be. In this book, Religion and Psychology work hand in hand, and often terms are translated from one language to the other. Many of the chapters fire the imagination, and they bear such titles as "The value of Confession," "The Romance of Unconscious Motives," "Don't be Tired Tomorrow," "The Curse and Cure of Impure Thoughts," and "The Soul's Urge to Completeness." There is also an appendix containing a Commentary on Christian Science and a Psychological Bibliography.

SECTION IV

RELIGION IN THE SOCIAL SCIENCES

A. ECONOMICS

Baum, Maurice (compiler and arranger). READINGS IN BUSINESS
ETHICS; A Survey of the Principles and Problems of American
Business Morality. Dubuque, Iowa: William C. Brown Company,
1950. Pp. viii 209   3.75

This volume brings together, in a careful and systematic arrange-
ment, selections from books, magazines and other publications, material which is pertinent to moral and ethical principles in Business and
Economics. Where there is a diversity of views possible, the compiler
attempts to balance opposite expressions of opinion. A preface and
Part I present what the writer is trying to do and outline the role of
moral principles—only recently the concern of American Business—
which are applicable to the development of the conscience of the
modern merchant and producer. Especially illustrative of attempts to
clean their own house are the efforts of various tradesmen and mer-
chandisers to formulate ethical codes applicable in their business.
Topic III of Part I deals with "Religion, Christianity, and Capitalistic
Ethics" with material drawn from the writings of Edward A. Filene,
Reinhold Niebuhr, the Amsterdam Assembly, and William A. Cham-
berlain. Though the codes formulated by each business as given are
primarily naturalistic in motivation, they do illustrate an awakening
sense of need for fairness and social fair-dealing. Other chapters of
significance deal with National and Local Better Business Bureaus,
the Ethical Problems of Selling, Ethical Problems of Competition, and
Ethical Problems of Advertising.

Bennett, John Coleman, and others. CHRISTIAN VALUES AND ECO-
NOMIC LIFE. New York: Harper and Brothers, 1954. Pp. 272.   3.50

Howard R. Bowen, William A. Brown, Jr. and Bishop G. Bromley
Oxnam, are the other contributors to this summary volume on Ethics
and Economic Life produced by the National Council of Churches.
In the Preface, Bennett expresses the hope that the study as a whole
may provide the most useful materials now available for the formation
of a Protestant economic ethic relevant to our situation.

Bishop Oxnam contributes a historical sketch which provides excellent background to the circumstances of the study and emphasizes his
own outlook that "Christians judge all economic systems by the im-
peratives of Christian faith . . . " Prof. Bowen, an economist, summarizes the findings of the study, listing eleven subordinate goals to the
overreaching aim of life which is made to be Christian love. William
A. Brown, Jr., another economist, brings into the picture "The Inter-

national Implications of Christian Economic Ethics." Finally, Bowen and Bennett conclude the summary with chapters on "Ethics and Economics" and "Christian Ethics in Economic Life."

Boulding, Kenneth E. THE ORGANIZATIONAL REVOLUTION; A Study in the Ethics of Economic Organization. New York: Harper and Brothers, 1953. Pp. xxxiv 286. 3.50

Boulding's analysis of the *Organizational Revolution* has been appraised by reviewers as being more sociological and political than economic. In the study are found occasional references to the influence of Religion in both an ethical and social sense. It brings into the picture the role of loyalty and the "minor virtues" such as honesty, truthfulness, sobriety, attentiveness to promises, and the like. At the end of the text there is a commentary by Reinhold Niebuhr entitled, "Coercion, Self-Interest, and Love" with the author's reply. This volume is the second in the series on Christian Ethics and Economic Life.

Bowen, Howard Rothmann. SOCIAL RESPONSIBILITIES OF THE BUSINESSMAN. New York: Harper and Brothers, 1953. Pp. 276. 3.50

In recent years religious leaders have recognized the urgency of the ethical problems of our economic life, and this volume of the series on Christian Ethics and Economic Life, directs its attention to the social responsibilities of the businessman. The early chapters of the book are directed to a proper understanding of social and economic goals, some modified by Christian ethics, and some not. F. Ernest Johnson of the National Council of Churches provides an "ethical critique" at the end of the book, relating the whole issue to the basic principles of Christian ethics and a sense of Christian vocation in daily work. Appendix A has a very useful "Bibliography of Protestant Views on the Social Responsibilities of the Businessman." Appendix B offers a partial list of businessmen who have published their conception of social responsibilities.

Childs, Marquis William, and Cater, Douglass. ETHICS IN A BUSINESS SOCIETY. New York: Harper and Brothers, 1954. Pp. 191. 2.75

Ethics in a Business Society supplements the studies originated in the Department of Church and Economic Life of the Federal Council of Churches, and later continued when that Council was joined with the National Council. This little book brings into Christian economic practices and ethics both interpretation and historical perspective. There is an easy to understand analysis of the philosophy of business and its goals in the various periods—Mediaeval, Renaissance, and Post-Renaissance—and an examination of the problem of conscience when some leaders of men have given thought to the goals of life.

Demant, Vigo Auguste. RELIGION AND THE DECLINE OF CAPITAL-
ISM. New York: Charles Scribner's Sons, 1952. Pp. 9 204. 3.00

In a historical sense, this volume is the antithesis of R. H. Tawney's
Religion and the Rise of Capitalism. Where Tawney's development
stopped with the Renaissance, Demant's begins with the nineteenth
century. "Capitalism" is made to denote one or all of these three
things: a form of economic organization, the mainspring of a certain
kind of culture, and an outlook on the relation of the material universe to human existence. In writing of the *decline* of capitalism, the
author is attempting to show how the principles which are associated
with capitalism, such as the *laissez-faire* market and the Manchester
School notion of "natural laws" of economy, have come increasingly
under social control. To the extent that the Christian sense of social
responsibility has displaced individual monopoly and irresponsibility,
capitalism has declined. The theological implications of the theme of
the book are drawn out in the last chapter: "God's Will and our
Modern Age."

Hoyt, Elizabeth Ellis. AMERICAN INCOME AND ITS USE. New York:
Harper and Brothers, 1954. Pp. xxi 362. 4.00

This fourth volume in the larger study of Christian Ethics and
Economic Life has as its most valuable chapter for those interested in
economic philosophy and religion, the conclusion: "What Lies Before
Us." Of pertinence to the theme is the opening chapter entitled
"Wealth and the Good Life," wherein Hoyt reviews varied views,
Oriental and Occidental, as to the purpose served by material wealth.
Dean Walter G. Muelder writes the commentary, with the title, "Ethi-
cal Aspects of Income Distribution and Consumption," with some 16
suggestions to the Churches in terms of what they can do to educate
their people on the subject.

Ryan, John Augustine. A LIVING WAGE, Its Ethical and Economic
Aspects. New York: Macmillan Company, 1906. Pp. xiii 361. (o.p.)

Does or does not the doctrine of wages rest upon a broad Christian
religious and ethical foundation? In this work, originally a PhD.
treatise in Economics, Ryan holds that the working man's wages
should be sufficiently high to enable him to live in a manner consistent with the dignity of a human being. While the data and the specific
facts given by the author have changed materially since the book was
written, the writer's principle of judgment—that the laborer has a
right to obtain a reasonably sufficient amount of the earth's product
to afford him a decent livelihood—is still worth considering. "The latter right is, like all other moral rights, based on his intrinsic worth as
a person, and on the sacredness of those needs that are essential to the
reasonable development of personality." Chapter XX contains the
author's "Summary and Conclusions." The author does not pretend
to force any particular verse of the Gospels to justify his view, but
bases his argument on general considerations. A helpful bibliography,

using the texts of the classical moralists as well as the turn of the century writers, is found at the end.

Stamp, Josiah Charles. CHRISTIANITY AND ECONOMICS. New York: Macmillan Company, 1938. Pp. x 194. 2.00 (o.p.)

A very sane and "practical" approach to the problem of the part Christianity is to play in economics is always greatly to be desired. This work, by a well-known English peer, presents the problem very sensibly and free from the high dreaming common to many other works.

In the Fifth Chapter, the preliminary conclusions are thus set down: (1) Christ's teaching had primarily a spiritual and not an economic bearing. As far as they went, its economics were directed to the conditions of His own time, which were quite different from those prevailing today. This alone makes it difficult to transfer his utterance literally to the circumstances of today. (2) Attempts made to derive direct economic guidance from the Scriptures have generally failed. (3) The Christian Scripture does not present or favor any particular form of economic or political society, or any plan of economic life. (4) The Christian impetus behind the moral betterment of the world, especially by its doctrines of pity, justice, and rights of the indiviual, has been largely responsible for certain prevailing conditions and undertones of business.

Chapter V, "The Fundamental Christian Principles," is informative and develops the idea that since Christian virtues are individual, they cannot be turned into statutes. "But, as they become more widely practical, institutions which are based on a presumption of their generality can be made to work on a higher plane."

Tawney, Richard Henry. RELIGION AND THE RISE OF CAPITALISM, A Historical Study. New York: Harcourt, Brace, and Company, 1926. Pp. x 337. 4.50

Not many writers on the history of economic thought and development and its connection with Religion have the knowledge and perspective which R. H. Tawney brings into the subject. The value of the volume is that it traces strands in the development of religious thought on social and economic questions as the Christian era passed from the mediaeval to the modern periods. It should be added that this book stops with the beginning of the eighteenth century, but even so, a foundation of much of modern religious and economic doctrine is to be found in the text. In his "conclusion" Prof. Tawney says: "The distinction made by the philosophers of classical antiquity between liberal and servile occupations, the mediaeval insistence that riches exist for man, not man for riches, Ruskins famous outburst, 'there is not wealth but life,' the argument of the Socialist who urges that production should be organized for service, not profit, are but different attempts to emphasize the instrumental character of economic activities by reference to an ideal which is held to express the true nature of man."

Ward, Alfred Dudley. THE GOALS OF ECONOMIC LIFE. New York:
Harper and Brothers, 1953. Pp. 470. 4.00

Goals of Economic Life is one of the six volume study of Christian
Ethics and Economic Life produced by a study committee of the National Council of Churches. Here each of fifteen writers, a specialist
in Economics, Political Science, Theology, Psychology, Anthropology
and others, attempt to assess the ethics of present-day economic goals.

This particular volume to many has appeared to be more valuable
for the diversity of opinion it represents on the same issues than an
encouraging sign of a coming agreement among Protestants on the
problem of Christianity in Economics. Some critics of the book feel
that the contributors have not examined the fundamental issue, and
have tended to accept and rationalize the traditional Protestant mores
rather than seek out Christian ethical standards of justice and the
Christian ethic of love. In some of the essays, too, material progress is
not clearly differentiated from moral goals. But the book will command the serious interest of those who have felt the serious need of
laying some foundations of the subject on which some building may
be done by those who follow and who understand the Christian Gospel as well as the economics of the day. Attention should be called to
such significant chapters as Donald Snygg's "The Psychological Basis
of Human Values," Theodore M. Green's "Secular Values and Religious Faith," and Reinhold Niebuhr's "The Christian Faith and Economic Life of Liberal Society." An excellent Index is very helpful.

Ward, Alfred Dudley. THE AMERICAN ECONOMY: ATTITUDES AND
OPINIONS. New York: Harper and Brothers, 1955. Pp. xx 199. 3.50

That the ideas and attitudes toward the daily work can be reflections of spiritual and moral goals is well illustrated in this volume,
the fifth in the series sponsored by the National Council of Churches.
This study was limited to some 500 professionally planned interviews
with a variety of people in a number of occupations, as well as nearly
forty scattered group discussions. The 110 questions asked individuals
took from one and one half to two hours to answer. Answers to the
questions reveal goals and the directions of men's hearts and minds,
and the book abounds with living statistics. Part I of the volume has
to do with "Work," while Part II deals with "Moral Standards and
Problems."

Ward, Harry Frederick. OUR ECONOMIC MORALITY AND ETHICS
OF JESUS. New York: Macmillan Company, 1929. Pp. ix 329. 1.35
(o.p.)

"The separation between religion and economics in the Western
world since the Reformation must be charged as much to the religion-
ists as to the economists and businessmen. Most of them have relig-
iously kept the practical affairs of life outside the house of the Lord,
so that now it seems to many people irreverent and almost sacrilegious
to deal with economic matters in sermon or prayer." Much has happened in the economic world since Prof. Ward wrote this volume, but

his thesis is worth understanding, in that it opposes other views on this subject of the relation between economic virtues and religious graces. Especially pertinent, too, is the discussion in Chapter VI of "The Chief End of Man."

B. HISTORY AND HISTORICAL PERSPECTIVE

Greene, Evarts B. RELIGION AND THE STATE; The Making and Testing of an American Tradition. New York: New York University Press, 1941. Pp. 172. 2.75

In this Phelps Lecture on Early American History, a historian examines the American cultural heritage in terms of its European roots, its tranplantation of European ideas and the factors of life in the new country which liberalized and modified the old traditions. Chapter VI, "The American Tradition Tested" brings the material up to date with accounts of the conflicting philosophies in recent history which have brought the issue into the open again. There are extensive book notices at the end for material dealt with in each chapter.

Hallowell, John Hamilton. MAIN CURRENTS IN MODERN POLITICAL THOUGHT. New York: Henry Holt and Company, 1950. Pp. ix 759. 6.75

The main currents in political philosophy since 1600 are interpreted in this publication. This study intended to supply the lack of other studies in this area by presenting philosophical and theological presuppositions. There are four sections to the book: Liberalism; Socialism; The Revolution of Nihilism; The Crisis of our Times. A sampling from Chapter 15, The Revolt Against Reason, will give the reader an illustration of materials within this book. The author makes a comparison between guilt as understood in Christianity in contrast to Freudian psychology.

Hallowell, John Hamilton. MORAL FOUNDATIONS OF DEMOCRACY. Chicago: University of Chicago Press, 1954. 3.50

This book presents the idea that democracy to be preserved requires reinforcement of Hebraic-Greek-Christian Faith. The writer presents the argument that "democratic politics ought to be a matter of ethical means directed toward rational ends."

Niebuhr, Reinhold. FAITH AND HISTORY. New York: Scribner's and Sons, 1949. Pp. viii 257. 3.50

Contrasts the classical, Biblical, and modern interpretation of history. A philosophical presentation of the idea that man has made exaggerated claims about himself. This exaggeration leads to complacency and despair. Solution, adopt "element Christian behavior in man's freedom of source of *both* evil *and* good. Mans need of redemption, and God's certain grace to work out solutions in a point of history yet unfathomed." Then hope can be restored.

Shinn, Roger L. CHRISTIANITY AND THE PROBLEM OF HISTORY.
Scribner's and Sons, 1953. Pp. 302. 4.50

This is a critical survey of the history of the philosophy of history.
The stress is upon eschatology. The views of Christian writers from
Augustine to Karl Barth, and Arnold Toynbee are presented.

Toynbee, Arnold Joseph. A STUDY OF HISTORY; An Abridgement of
Volumes I-VI, by D. C. Somervell. New York: Oxford University
Press, 1947. Pp. xiii 617. 6.00

Toynbee's views of history are widely known, and though in some
cases widely criticized, are in many ways unique and likely to be read
for many years to come. He seems to be among the very few historians
who in his analysis of the rise and decline of civilizations, has given a
very prominent part to the influence of Religion. His extensive study
of History now covers ten volumes, and this book is an abridgement
of the first six. The questions he asked with reference to the history
of England are typical and can be applied to the history of any other
nation. "Is English history intelligible when taken by itself? Can we
abstract an internal history of England from her external relations?
If we can, shall we find that these residual external relations are of
secondary importance? . . ." Toynbee writes history with a Platonic
and religious perspective. The plan of this book is to illustrate the
geneses, growth, and disintegration of civilizations, and the especially
fascinating notion of "The Rhythm of Civilizations."

C. POLITICAL SCIENCE AND GOVERNMENT

Callender, Clarence N., and Charlesworth, James C. (editors). ETHICAL
STANDARDS IN AMERICAN PUBLIC LIFE. Philadelphia: American Acadamy of Political and Social Science, 1952. Pp. x 255. 2.00

"Political maturity," say the editors in the Foreword, "connotes a
high standard of ethics in government, regardless what the level may
be in business or private life, and the community is entitled to insist
that all public servants accept the fact." In this collection of nineteen
articles a spokesman for each of a wide range of subjects having ethical implications has been invited to express his views. The subject
matter has five divisions, with articles under each: Patterns of Public
Morality, Ethical Standards in Public Elections, Ethical Standards in
Governmental Agencies, Sources of Influence and Pressure, and the
Measurement and Promotion of Ethical Standards. Senator Kefauver
writes the initial article on "Past and Present Standards of Public
Ethics in America: Are we Improving?" Profs. Howard Bowen and
Joseph A. Loftus contribute articles on "How Public Spirited is
American Business?" and, similarly, "Labor." F. Ernest Johnson and
Ralph Himstead contribute, "Do Churches Exert Significant Influence
on Public Morality?" and "The Colleges, Ethics, and the Public,"
respectively. There are other significant articles by Charles P. Taft and
Senator Paul Douglass. In the main, it is an excellent collection of
serious essays which reflects current thinking and concern.

Chandler, Albert Richard. THE CLASH OF POLITICAL IDEALS: A Source Book on Democracy, Communism and the Totalitarian State. New York: D. Appleton-Century Company, 1940. Pp. xvii 273. 2.75

There is this quotation from the *Communist Manifesto*: "The charges against Communism made from a religious, a philosophical, and generally, from an ideological standpoint, are not deserving of serious examination. Does it require deep intuition to comprehend that man's ideas, views, and conceptions, in one word, man's consciousness, changes with every change in his material existence, in his social relations, and in his social life? . . . The ruling ideas of each age have ever been the ideas of its ruling class . . ." Chandler has chosen material from documents which are sources for various political and socio-economic philosophies, and allowed them to represent themselves. There are selections from Thucydides on the Athenian Democracy, Locke on Civil Government and Jefferson on Democracy. Washington writes on Freedom, Unity, and Peace. Material from John Stuart Mill, Lincoln and Walt Whitman, Dewey on Progressive Democracy, the text of the "Communist Manifesto," are included. Marxism in the Twentieth Century by Lenin and Stalin, Mussolini and Hitler are quoted on Fascism and Nazism respectively; while the ideals at work in Japan prior to World War II, the Encyclical of Pope Pius XI on Reconstructing the Social Order, and an Epilogue titled "American Aspirations, 1940" help round out the picture.

Douglas, Paul Howard. ETHICS IN GOVERNMENT. Cambridge, Mass.: Harvard University Press, 1952. Pp. ix 114. 2.25

In this Godkin Lecture at Harvard University, Senator Douglass of Illinois, undertakes a diagnosis of our political moral standards. The basis of some of his judgments is the number of disclosures brought to light by Congressional investigating committees from 1950-1952. In the chapter on the "Ethical Problems of Administrators," Senator Douglas argues that there is less corruption in a free market, where prices are fixed by the law of supply and demand; state regulation invites pressure and bribery. Among his recommendations for improvement he would list a mandatory disclosure of private income for all legislators; a second would be to make their investments as distinct from their government obligations as possible. On a higher plane, he urges the need for personal codes of honor and deeper individual moral values. "Since the state is the individual writ large, perhaps the disclosures of the past years may reawaken within us a sense of our individual failure, to live up to the standards we inwardly cherish. The faults which we see in government are all too often the reflection of our own moral failures."

Ebersole, Luke Eugene. CHURCH LOBBYING IN THE NATION'S CAPITAL. New York: Macmillan Company, 1951. Pp. x 195. 2.75

Church Lobbying in the Nation's Capital is a very real answer to any who may think that the various bodies of churches preach only the Kingdom of God. The author says his purpose is "to investigate church lobbying as a developing institution of organized religion, to set forth its organization, to view its practices, to survey the interests around which it centers, and to discover the changes which it is undergoing." There are chapters on "Protestant Lobbies," "Catholic Lobbies," and "Methods of Church Lobbying." There is no implication that all lobbying is wrong. The writer presents his material objectively and often in terms of quotations from published press releases. There are lobbies which represent individual denominations, such as Methodists, Congregationalists, Quakers, *et al.*, and there are lobbies which are collective. The methods of lobbying vary from helping to draft platforms and influencing nominations and elections to furnishing information and bringing pressures upon congressmen. Material of special interest has to do with public education, and at times the obvious propaganda which masquerades as a protective interest. The concluding chapter draws threads together and shows what general interests and diverse elements are at work at the present time. Of interest, too, is the extent of lobbying involving separation of church and state.

Gerhart, Eugene C. AMERICAN LIBERTY AND "NATURAL LAW."
    Boston: Beacon Press, 1953. Pp. 212. 3.00

"Natural Law" is placed in quotation marks to reflect the view of the author that by and large, it is an undefinable term. In the book there are many views of natural law, and Mr. Gerhart is especially concerned to see that whatever view is adopted or adapted does not leave out the sovereignty of the people. Perhaps the most pointed chapter is that entitled "Church and State—The Papal View versus the Traditional American View." Here the discussion contrasts the views on government, "lawful authority," and moral as against "natural" law. Much is made of the philosophy of the encyclical letter, *Immortale Dei* of Pope Leo XIII, and its views on the sources of authority are contrasted with those expressed by Jefferson in his "Act for Establishing Religious Freedom" (1786) which was based on what he called "The natural rights of mankind." The book contains a Selected Bibliography dealing with the legal aspects of separation of ecclesiastical and political authority, and copious notes. Dean Roscoe Pound of the Harvard Law School writes an Introduction to it.

Hyma, Albert. CHRISTIANITY AND POLITICS, A History of the
    Principles and Struggles of Church and State. Philadelphia: J. B.
    Lippincott Company, 1938. Pp. ii 331. 3.00 (o.p.)

Though prepared as a companion to the author's earlier *Christianity, Capitalism and Communism,* this volume carries forward the theme of the relationship of orthodox Christianity to political life up to the present time. The initial chapter compares the Church and State in the Middle Ages, and the text ends with a summary of the role of Christianity in Democracy such as is established in the United States. The principle of religious freedom and the operation of the kindred principle of the separation of church and state receive incidental treatment.

Keller, James Gregory. YOU CAN CHANGE THE WORLD; The Christopher Approach. New York: Longmans, Green and Company, 1948. Pp. vix 387. 3.00

"Each Christopher carries Christ with him, individually and personally, into the dust and heat of the marketplace, into the highways as well as the byways, thereby helping to change for the better the trends abroad in the world today." And each Christopher is bidden to Pray for All, Go to All, and Teach All. Father Keller's now well-known Christopher Movement aims at counteracting the evil in social and political life not by crusading hostility, but by militant love. "People are won or lost by ideas, *not by things,*" says the author. This book is said to be a guide book or textbook for the use of Christophers. The ideas found within the book are simple as homespun and very much down-to-earth. Their emphasis is on personal initiative and responsibility; leavening the whole lump by personal example. There is little dogma or preaching, but hardly a page does not relate personal action to the examples set down in the Christian Gospels.

MacIver, Robert Morrison (editor). CONFLICTS OF LOYALTIES; A Series of Addresses and Discussion. New York: Harper and Brothers, 1952. Pp. vii 150. 2.00

Each of these eleven essays was a lecture given at the Institute of Religious and Social Studies of the Jewish Theological Seminary in 1950-51. A wide variety of subjects are considered, some with intriguing titles. Thus, Lyman Bryson considers the full implications of Democracy in his "On Deceiving the Public for the Public Good." Roger N. Baldwin discusses "The Justifiable Grounds of Disobedience to Law,"—a subject considered from another side by Franz L. Neumann, with his "On the Limits of Justifiable Disobedience." Liston Pope writes a provocative essay about "Making Friends with the Hammon of Unrighteousness." The second portion of the book has to do with the Some Conflicts of our Times. W. W. Waymack here writes about the Hiroshima Issue and its implications for civilization; Dr. Louis Finkelstein writes on "Institutionalism and Faith"; and there is an essay on "Freedom and Interference in American Education" by Ordway Tead. At the end of the book there are to be found brief paragraph biographies of the contributors.

Osgniach, Augustine John. THE CHRISTIAN STATE. Milwaukee: Bruce Publishing Company, 1943. Pp. xix 356 (o.p.)

This volume expounds the Roman Catholic philosophy of the ends toward which the Christian State is directed and which civil society helps man to attain, i. e., realization of the purpose for which God has created him. The educational philosophy of the state is developed in detail in an appropriate chapter as are also the rights of the church to teach the truth of salvation to every human being. Chapters of especial interest are "The Natural Basis of Society and the State," "The Purpose and Function of the State," and "The Family and The State." There are supplementary readings at the end of each chapter and an extensive General Bibliography.

Rogers, Edward. A CHRISTIAN COMMENTARY ON COMMUNISM. New York: Frederick A. Prager, Inc., 1952. Pp. 238.   3.50

"This book, written by a British Methodist clergyman, is an uncommonly readable and lucid analysis which gives evidence of scholarly research and comprehension. The author is convinced of the incompatibility of Communism and Christianity, both in fundamental assumptions and in methods of procedure . . . using the historical approach, he begins with evidences of Communism in classical society and traces its emergence and practice among the early Christians and the fairly rapid disposal of it by the Church Fathers. It was the renaissance and the 'eclipse of theology' which promoted once again a confidence that man was capable of creating the good society on earth and that the trend of evolution assured his success.

"Following the introductory chapters, the major portion of the book is concerned with modern Communism. The author skillfully guides one through the mazes of philosophical concept and economic theory which, through the extraordinary brain and personality of Karl Marx, evolved into the doctrines of Communism. He also explicates the radical changes in interpretation and emphasis which occurred in the 'great experiment' in Russia. It is evident that no generalization concerning 'Communism' is wholly valid unless one defines the brand of Communism to which he is referring . . . "Christianity, with a more realistic acceptance of the sinfulness and fallibility of man, does not expect the formation of a perfect society on earth, but it does set the vitally important concerns of this world in the context of eternity . . . In a sense, Communism is one of the world's greatest heresies, which would not have arisen if the church had preached and lived the full gospel." From the review by Murray H. Leiffer, in *Religious Education*, XLVIII (Nov.-Dec., 1953).

D. SOCIOLOGY AND SOCIAL MOVEMENTS

Casserley, Julien Victor Langmead. MORALS AND MAN IN THE SOCIAL SCIENCES. New York: Longmans, Green, and Company, 1951. Pp. ix 230.   3.50

Dr. Casserley's thesis is that in its quest of enduring ideals, essentially philosophic in character, Sociology need not sacrifice its scientific objectivity. He describes the sociologist's activity as "a quest, through the relativities of social life for those absolute necessities of social life which the relativities assimilate, accommodate, disguise and conceal, but nevertheless embody and express." The whole study is projected against a background of historical philosophy and Christian social relations, so that the writer may "explore the role of the relative in Christianity and the possibility of the absolute in sociology." Like most scholars trained in Europe, his knowledge of philosophy and history is extensive.

Of especial interest are the chapters on "The Origins and Axioms of Modern Sociology," where he does a service by keeping separate Sociology, the science of principles from the surveys, statistics, and empirical data which are really its tools; and that on "Types of

49

Humanism" in which he shows the human worth of the principles discovered in the natural sciences when these are applied to sociological matters.

Cook, Lloyd Allen, and Cook, Elaine F. INTERGROUP EDUCATION. New York: McGraw Hill Book Company, 1954. Pp. 392. 5.50

Intergroup Education is explained by the authors to be the same as intercultural education,—the bringing together, into a cultural harmony diverse races and creeds by the democratic process of sharing each other's thoughts and ideals and eventually achieving better understanding with each other. In the book is a statement of the goals (p. 14) and a number of chapters which present the various features of the subject: e.g., Minorities in the Light of History, Group Relations in Early Childhood, College Campus—Views and Values, Adult Community—Caste and Class, Teach World Unity to Youth, and The Educator's Role. The emphasis is primarily social and sociological, but there is some attention given to teaching about religion. At the end of each chapter is a list of selected readings.

Hughley, Judge Neal. TRENDS IN PROTESTANT SOCIAL IDEALISM. New York: King's Crown Press, 1948. Pp. xiii 184. 3.00

The material included in this book is limited to contemporary American Protestant thought, and only certain samples of that thought. The author is careful to state that the samples represented in the treatment are not the only intellectual patterns. Not considered are European Thought, and American Jewish and American Catholic views. The author says: "What we seek is a description and an analysis of the most recent development in social philosophy emanating from certain theological sources in America."

An initial chapter considers "The Heritage of the Social Gospel, and the last chapter is on "Neo-Protestantism vs. Social Gospel Idealism." Sandwiched in-between are studies on E. Stanley Jones in terms of "Kingdom of God Idealism"; Charles A. Ellwood and "Christian Sociology"; Francis J. McConnell and "Religious-Democratic Reformism"; Kirby Page and "Christian-Pacific Socialism": Harry F. Ward and "Christian Marxism," and Reinhold Niebuhr and "Dialectical Theological Socialism." The material is well documented from original sources, and at the end of the volume there is an excellent Bibliography giving the titles of books pertinent to the matter discussed in the several chapters.

Hutchison, John Alexander (editor). CHRISTIAN FAITH AND SOCIAL ACTION. New York: Charles Scribner's Sons, 1953. Pp. 246. 3.50

"This volume is inspired by and dedicated to Reinhold Niebuhr by his former students,, colleagues and friends who have been members of the Frontier Fellowship . . .

The most helpful and incisive chapters of the book for this reviewer are the following: Hutchison's neat recital of the development of the Fellowship, also giving much information of the development of social Christianity; Lehman's careful attempt to lay a foundation for a distinctively Christian ethic; Tillich's customary masterful handling of the placing of persons in a technical culture; Heimann's difficult and full treatment of freedom and totalitarianism; Holloway's exceptionally well informed analysis of the wrong turnings in Protestantism's effort to meet or escape responsibility in foreign affairs; Herberg's suggestive exploration of the relation of faith and secular learning, and Niebuhr's retrospective and prospective statement on Christian faith and social action . . ."

From the review by Clyde A. Holbrook in *Religious Education*, XLIX (Jan.-Feb., 1954) .

May, Henry Farnham. PROTESTANT CHURCHES AND INDUSTRIAL AMERICA. New York: Harper and Brothers, 1949. Pp. x 297. 3.50

Whether pleasing to all or not, America has become a predominantly industrial nation, and this book attempts to portray the impact of a Protestant "bloc" of churches—Presbyterian, Congregationalist, Baptist, Methodist, and Episcopalian—on the social life in America. Actually, this volume is a study of the social-religious history as it was shaped during the century of industrialization and covers from 1828 to the termination of the 19th century. About one-half of the volume is devoted to a study of "Social Christianity," the theological thought and ideals which produced what has since come to be known as "The Social Gospel." There is an extensive 24-page Bibliography at the end which is devoted to books of current religious-social interest.

Neill, Thomas Patrick. RELIGION AND CULTURE; THE CHRISTIAN IDEA OF MAN IN CONTEMPORARY SOCIETY. Milwaukee: Bruce Publishing Company, 1952. Pp. 102. 2.75

"This is a very refreshing and stimulating book. There is nothing narrow or dogmatic about the approach to the subject. It is, in fact, encouraging that the author so frequently refers to prominent Protestant writers and is not reluctant in seeing the Holy Spirit at work in Non-Catholic circles.

Dr. Neill is a distinguished and brillant scholar who writes in a very facile and easy style. After clearly establishing the premise that the culture of Western civilization is primarily Christian, he reveals how it has gradually disintegrated under the impact of the secularism of the day. As it was impossible within the compass of so small a book to discuss all important doctrines of the church, Dr. Neill has limited himself to a consideration of the Christian view of man claiming that it is 'probably the most influential of all Christian ideas in molding Western culture . . .' "

From the review by (Rev.) John Schott, in *Religious Education*, XLIX (July-August, 1954) .

Niebuhr, Reinhold. DOES CIVILIZATION NEED RELIGION? A Study in the Social Resources and Limitations of Religion in Modern Life. New York: Macmillan Company, 1928. Pp. 242. 2.00 (o.p.)

"Whatever may be said of specific religions and religious forms," says the author, "it is difficult to imagine man without religion: for religion is the champion of personality in a seemingly impersonal world. It prompts man to organize his various impulses . . . into a moral unity; it persuades him, when its vitality is unimpaired, to regard his fellows with an appreciation commensurate with his own self-respect; and it finally discovers and creates a universe in which the human spirit is guaranteed the security against the forces of nature which always seem to reduce it to a mere effervescence unable to outlast the collocation of forces which produce it." In this commentary, Dr. Niebuhr considers the nature of the forces which are pitted against Religion (such as Nature and Civilization), the "Social Resources of Religion," "Religion and Life: Conflict and Compromise," and "A Philosophy for an Ethical Religion." The essay is a worthwhile background for any study of the social medium in which Religion is rooted.

Nottingham, Elizabeth Kristine. RELIGION AND SOCIETY. Garden City, New York: Doubleday Short Studies in Sociology, 1954. Pp. 84. 1.00

This brief study is intended to be an *introduction* to the study of the Sociology of Religion. It seeks to avoid theology and to base its examination on a *functional* analysis and interpretation of religion in social movements and social motivations. The author says that "Religion is treated in a broad and universal sense, from a social rather than an individual or theological standpoint. Our inquiry is focused on its functions in furthering or hampering the survival and maintenance of social groups." It is also made clear that the writer respects the inspirational force of religion and tries to see it in its best aspects as a cohesive and conserving force in a social structure.

A merit of the book is that the author avoids iconoclasm, and even if her concern with religion is only with its function rather than its truth, she tries to see religion in its best social service.

Sherrington, Charles Scott. MAN ON HIS NATURE. London: Cambridge University Press, 1951 (second edition). Pp. 300. 6.00

An eminent English physiologist considers the nature of man from its foundations in the physical life and "the wisdom of the body" to its apex in the mind. *Man on his Nature,* given originally as the Gifford Lectures, shows how closely the more eminent scientists are relating the laws of the physical world and the world of mind. The evolution of the organism moves from the realm where personal survival is paramount to the realm where the quality of altruism is the inspiration behind motive actions. "We think back . . . to that ancient biological pre-human scene whence, so we have learned, we came; there *no* life was a sacred thing . . . For man, the situation has changed . . . The change is in himself. Where have his 'values' come from? The infra-human life he escaped from knew them not . . . He is slowly drawing from life the inference that altruism, charity, is a duty incumbent upon thinking life." There are very informative chapters on "The Wisdom of the Body," "The Brain and its Work," and "Brain Collaborates with Psyche."

52

Sweet, William Warren. RELIGION IN THE DEVELOPMENT OF AMERICAN CULTURE, 1765-1840. New York: Charles Scribner's Sons, 1952. Pp. xiv 338. 3.50

The central theme of the book is the part played by organized religion in the westward movement of the population of America. While the volume is primarily concerned with the adjustments to the frontier made by various Christian denominations, much of the material is of interest to educators and education inasmuch as where the religious groups became entrenched, schools and colleges were established which reflected their views of life and reality. Of especial interest are the chapters having to do with "Religion Follows the Frontier" and "Barbarism vs. Revivalism." "Frontier Utopias," such as Mormonism, the Shakers, the Rappites, and various Millenial Sects are dealt with in the last chapter. There is a very extensive Bibliography of source material which includes references to books, magazine articles, and unpublished doctoral dissertations.

Troeltsch, Ernst. THE SOCIAL TEACHING OF THE CHRISTIAN CHURCHES. New York: Macmillan and Company, 1931 (two volumes). Pp. 13-445; 445-1019. 10.50

Troeltsch's work on the subject is encyclopedic and exhaustive. The first volume analyzes the social teaching and motivations of early and mediaeval Christianity. The second is devoted to Protestantism and the Protestant denominations. The author says that the two periods represent different points of view: the first conceives of Christian fellowship as an institution (the Church), not dependent on individualism and possessing a deposit of absolute truths and sacramental powers; the second, conceives of Christian fellowship as a society whose life is constantly renewed by the deliberate allegiance and personal work of its individual members. Thus, this second volume attempts an exhaustive treatment of the second conception. There are chapters on "The Sociological Problem of Protestantism," "Lutheranism," "Calvinism," and what is called "The Sect-Type and Mysticism within Protestantism."

RELIGION IN THE NATURAL SCIENCES

A. THE PHILOSOPHY OF SCIENCE

Barnes, Ernest William. SCIENTIFIC THEORY AND RELIGION, The World Described by Science and Its Spiritual Interpretation. New York: Macmillan Company, 1933. Pp. xxiv 686.   4.00 (o.p.)

These chapters were given originally as the Gifford Lectures, in 1927-29 by the Bishop of Birmingham, who holds several Science degrees in his own rights. In the Introduction, the author tells us he believes that "the scientific conception of the world leads us to postulate the guidance of a single controlling Intelligence. The philosophic view, termed Naturalism, suffices when we merely *describe* phenomena. To explain them we need to assume the existence of a unifying and directing Mind." In sum, "Theology cannot be based solely on human spiritual intelligence: it must take into account the experiences of the God of Nature revealed by science." The philosophical assumption of the lecturer is that of "moderate idealism" (his phrase),—that the physical world exists independently of any human mind. We are informed that the material is intended for educated men and women who have no technical knowledge of science or philosophy, and the general ideas of the author form a coherent and intelligible whole even if the descriptions of technical matters occasionally introduced by the author are overlooked by the reader. The book covers a vast panorama, with chapters on "Matter," "Space," "Space-Time: The Special Theory of Relativity," "The Electrical Theory of Matter," "The Solar System," "The Origin of Life and the Geological Record," various chapters on Evolution, "Scientific Theory and the Real World," "God and Our Belief in His Existence," the various aspects of "Religious Experience" and "Immortality." He concludes with the observation that "the world is full of surprises and perplexities: but it is not a Chaos. There is order within it . . . Behind the world, controlling Nature, is the Creative Spirit to Whom we are somehow akin . . ."

Eddington, Arthur Stanley. SCIENCE AND THE UNSEEN WORLD. New York: Macmillan Company, 1930. Pp. 91.   .75

In this Swarthmore Lecture, delivered before the Yearly Meeting of Quakers, in London, 1929, an eminent English professor of Astronomy sets forth his views on the direction of modern science, and the connection between the spirit of science and the spirit of religion. Speaking as both a scientist and a Quaker, he says that, "Religious creeds are a great obstacle to any full sympathy between the outlook of the scientist and the outlook which religion is so often supposed to require . . . Quakerism, in dispensing with creeds, holds out a hand to the scientist. "And lest he be misunderstood, he adds that, "Rejection of the creeds is not inconsistent with being possessed by a living belief . . . If our so-called facts are changing shadows, they are shadows cast by the light of constant truth."

Heim, Karl. THE TRANSFORMATION OF THE SCIENTIFIC WORLD VIEW. New York: Harper and Brothers, 1953. Pp. 262. 3.50

"If we wish to investigate the relation between faith in God and the theses of modern natural science," says the author, "we require an origin from which to plot the inquiry, just as a circle must have its origin immovably fixed in order that the circumference may be plotted in a given plane. The fixed point from which we must begin can be none other than God." This volume is written from a wide background in science and theology, and owes much of its inspiration to the teachings of Martin Luther. The writer says that "the collapse of a casual mechanical world-picture has again made room for God. Well-known scientists have committed themselves to the view that the marvellous constitution of the world's structure not only permits the inference of an intelligent Creator, but invites such an inference." In the book there are valuable insights and discussions of such matters as Materialism and a Religious Faith, the varied aspects of the Theory of Relativity, the concept of Casual Necessity, and the problem of Miracles in the light of Modern Natural Science. The last chapter discusses Mechanism and Vitalism.

Hocking, William Ernest. SCIENCE AND THE IDEA OF GOD. Chapel Hill: University of North Carolina Press, 1944. Pp. ix 124. 1.50

This series of lectures, delivered at the University of North Carolina, revolves around "an assumption which is plausible, which many believe to be true, which many believe is required by science, that we not only can, but must dispense with the traditional belief in God . . . I believe that trying it out is one of the best ways of seeing that it is not true." Hocking calls this procedure "a mental experiment in defective assumptions." The volume includes a chapter on "Science and Religion Today," and others on Science and its affects where meaning, purpose, and a conception of God make much difference. The direction of the needed sublimation of human desires is considered in the chapter on "Psychology and the Cure of Souls." Other significant chapters cover "Sociology and Humanism," and "Astronomy, Physics, and World-Meaning." In sum, concludes the author, "The human mind would have far less trouble with the idea of God if it were not persuaded that to be real is to act, and that to act is to have discoverable effects . . . God is a doer of deeds, a worker in history, a factor in the affairs of men . . ."

Russell, Bertrand. RELIGION AND SCIENCE. New York: Oxford University Press, 1935. Pp. 256. 2.00

Russell's views on the subject are well summarized at the end of the chapter on "Science and Ethics": I conclude, that while it is true that science cannot decide questions of value, that is because they cannot be intellectually decided at all and lie outside the realm of truth and falsehood. Whatever knowledge is attainable must be attained by the scientific methods; and whatever science cannot discover, mankind cannot know. "The volume develops Russell's thesis further. The book is not an objective account of the subject matter, nor is the author restrained in the traditional British sense; his own views are frequently intruded and the traditional and the revealed are often called on to justify themselves. At the end of the book the impression is left that the author's idea was to show Science and Religion in terms of their conflicts. " . . Since Copernicus, whenever science and theology have disagreed, science has proved victorious . . . The spread of the scientific outlook, as opposed to the theological, has indisputably made, hitherto, for happiness."

B. CHEMISTRY AND PHYSICS

Whitehead, Alfred North. CONCEPT OF NATURE. London: Macmillan and Company, 1920. Pp. viii 202. 4.25

In the Tarner Lectureship Endowment, the lecturers were to deliver a course on "The Philosophy of the Sciences and the Relations or Want of Relations between the different Departments of Knowledge." Whitehead says that his purpose is to lay the basis of a natural philosophy which is the necessary presupposition of a recognized speculative physics; it is an attempt to see a science usually thought of as limited to space and time, such as Physics, in terms of its higher meanings and relationships.

C. CONNECTED WITH VARIOUS ASPECTS OF MATHEMATICS

Coulson, Charles Alfred. SCIENCE AND CHRISTIAN BELIEF. Chapel Hill: University of North Carolina Press, 1955. Pp. 127. 2.50

It is the design of this McNair Lecture by an Oxford Professor of Mathematics to show how science has grown up *within* the Christian tradition. The writer has a very broad grasp of the history of science and marshals his facts with convincing force. He quotes approvingly a statement by the physicist, Heisenberg, that "It is for me easier to suppose that there are causes that elude and must forever elude our search, rather than to suppose that there are no causes at all . . . In short, we must admit causes beyond our comprehension. The electron leads to the doorway of religion." In this lecture, Coulson says that he will show that science is esssentially a religious activity, and in the last chapter, "Christian Belief," he carries this theme to a high point of reconciliation. "All life is sacramental; all nature is needed that

Christ should be understood: Christ is needed that all nature should be seen as holy . . ."

Whitehead, Alfred North. ESSAYS IN SCIENCE AND PHILOSOPHY. New York: Philosophical Library, Inc., 1947. Pp. vi 348. 4.75

This series of essays covers a multitude of subjects, for, Whitehead was not only a mathematician, but a man of broad scientific and humanistic background. Part II of the book has five essays on "Philosophy," Part III six essays on "Education," and the last Part, essays on "Science." Each of the essays has a depth and freshness which was characteristic of the man,—scientific yet not limited by science. There are thought-provoking essays on "Mathematics and the Good," "An Analysis of Meaning," "Mathematics and Liberal Education," "Process and Reality," "Science and General Education," "The Axioms of Geometry," and "Non-Euclidean Geometry." Among other values, Prof. Whitehead's essays enable the student to see everyday subjects; such as Mathematics and Education, in a meaningful perspective.

D. BIOLOGY AND ZOOLOGY

Drummond, Henry. NATURAL LAW IN THE SPIRITUAL WORLD. New York: A. L. Burt Company, 1926. 1.25 (o.p.)

Drummond's volume, which ran into many editions at the end of the century, is included primarily because of the unparalled way in which he made Science speak the language of the Bible, and for the Bible to speak the language of Science. Modern science has come much farther than the science of Darwin and Huxley and the Victorians which Drummond spoke to in his generation. Drummond's thesis is that "When any two phenomena in the two spheres (natural and 'supernatural') are seen to be analogous, the parallelism must depend upon the fact that the Laws governing them are not analogous, but identical." The student will find a "biology of the spirit" and the contention that the writers of the New Testament, especially, were driven to use the terminology of embryology and biology in comparing the birth of the "new man" because such terms are the only ones which will fit the situation. Chapters of especial significance which build upon the law of analogy are those dealing with "Degeneration," "Death," "Mortification," "Parasitism," "Semi-Parasitism," and "Conformity to Type."

Du Noüy, Pierre Lecomte. HUMAN DESTINY. New York: Longman's Green, and Company, 1947. Pp. xix 289. 3.75

Human Destiny is a thought-provoking blend of Biology and Philosophy. Its author is an internationally known French scientist and thinker, and in this volume physical science assumes philosophical dimensions and rises into Religion. The author says that "Evolution continues in our time, no longer on the physiological or anatomical plane, but on the spiritual and moral plane." To describe the goal of human evolution in teleological terms, Du Noüy coined the term "tele-finalism." This evolution is a progressive shedding of the animal and attainment of spirituality. "Spiritual thought personified by Jesus, does not seem to have gained either in depth or on the surface. This was to be expected, for it can only develop in beings who have already attained an advanced degree of moral perfection . . . it represents the supreme goal of humanity. Human evolution . . . depends above all on the progress of morality . . . If humanity makes this effort, it will contribute to the advent of the superior conscience preparatory to the pure and spiritual race destined to appear one day." Some chapters reflecting the views of the author, are Chapter xiii, "True Religion is in the Heart," and Chapter xv, "Education and Instruction."

Haldane, John Scott. THE SCIENCES AND PHILOSOPHY. Garden City, New York: Doubleday Doran and Company, Inc., 1929. Pp. x 330. 3.75 (o.p.)

In these Gifford Lectures at the University of Glasgow, Haldane tries to view the natural sciences in terms of philosophical perspective and significance. His own view he describes as "realistic" rather than "idealistic," and he tries to appraise the worth and and limitations of both mechanistic and vitalistic theories. In the chapter on "Philosophy, Religion and Theology," he says that without the aid of philosophy, any scientist is likely to be overborne by the apparent physical world and thus to obtain a distorted view of life. A chapter which rises to religious heights is entitled "The Belief in Immortality." Here the statement is found that "The argument of these lectures is that the physical world is not the real world, but only an ideal and quite insufficient representation of it. The real world is the spiritual world of values, and these values are in ultimate analysis nothing but the manifestation of the Supreme Spiritual Reality called, in the language of Religion, God."

Mason, Frances Baker (editor). CREATION BY EVOLUTION; A Consensus of Present Day Knowledge as Set forth by Leading Authorities in Non-Technical Language that all may understand. New York: Macmillan Company, 1928. Pp. xx 392. 5.00 (o.p.)

These essays by prominent scientists, English and American, may serve the teacher who has interest or needs to bring to the attention of others, material having to do with religion and science, not in terms of their warfare, but as allies against unbelief. "The book does not attempt to explain the origin of life," says the editor, "or to determine the causes which lie behind the changes in living things from age to age. It attempts to show that there are changes, and to describe how they came about. The revelation of creation by evolution which comes to us through science, widens and exalts our outlook on life and our religious faith, and these papers have been assembled in the hope that they may lead to a more general understanding of Nature and Nature's Way." An attempt is made in the book to give a new meaning to the word *evolution*: "It is far more than the unfolding of something which already exists . . evolution is the incessant appearance of new qualities, new characters, new powers, new beauties, for which there is no antecedent in experience or no evident promise in the germ itself."

There are chapters with these titles: "Evolution—Its Meaning," by David Starr Jordan; "Why We Must be Evolutionists" by J. Arthur Thompson; "Can We See Evolution Occuring?"; "Connecting and Missing Links in the Ascent to Man" by Richard S. Lull; and "The Mind in Evolution" by C. Lloyd Morgan. There are in all twenty-four chapters, contributed by leaders in various fields, with suggested readings at the end of each chapter and very choice quotations both appropriate to and expressive of a scientific and reverent spirit.

Sinnott, Edmund Ware. CELL AND PSYCHE; The Biology of Purpose. Chapel Hill: University of North Carolina Press, 1950. Pp. 121. 2.00

"What course a man will follow, or a nation, is set in no small measure by his basic creed about what he really thinks about the true nature of a human being—his personality, his freedom, his destiny, his relation to others and to the rest of the universe; by the judgments he makes as to what qualities and courses of action are admirable and should command his allegiance . . . The answer a man gives to them, is the most significant thing that one can know about him," so says the author in his Introduction. This little volume is a significant attempt to see Biology in human perspective, as revealing something of the direction of man's life and destiny. The material was delivered as a McNair Lecture at the University of North Carolina, and is divided into three parts: Part I, "Organization, The Distinctive Character of All Life"; Part II, "Biological Organization and Psychological Activity"; and Part III, "Some Implications for Philosophy."

Sinnott, Edmund Ware. TWO ROADS TO TRUTH. New York: Viking Press, Incorporated, 1953. Pp. 241. 3.50

The two roads to truth, according to Sinnott, are science and religion. However he does not see complete reconciliation between the two roads. He proposes a way how the two, science and religion, can have acceptable relationships.

Sinnott, Edmund Ware. BIOLOGY OF THE SPIRIT. New York: Viking Press, Incorporated, 1955. Pp. 180. 3.50

This book is a continuation of other works of Sinnott. The author proposes that protoplasm has biological purpose. He ties or integrates universal reality with the purposes of protoplasm. He illustrates his thesis with many examples from the field of biology.

RELIGION IN PROFESSIONAL EDUCATION

A. THE PRINCIPLES OF EDUCATION

Agnesine, Sister M. TEACHING RELIGION FOR LIVING. Milwaukee: Bruce Publishing Company, 1952. Pp. 184.

"The chief purpose of this book is to awaken in the religion teacher an awareness of his sublime calling: to teach the truths of our holy religion with so much warmth, sincerity and conviction, that pupils will want to accept and live these truths, and be impelled to share them with others." This volume is very practical and "challenging." As the writer remarks, the reader will often be confronted with problems and questions he must think through himself, and the book is intended to stimulate thought on certain things. There are thoughtful chapters on "What is Wrong with our Teaching," "Deepening the Impression Through Activity," and also many pages on tools and supplementary materials for "Evaluating our Teaching." Part III, is directed to problems and teaching situations which are more specific, as, teaching preparation for the Mass, Confession, How to Pray, and teaching Religion to Public School Children. There are books for reference at the end of each chapter and a longer list of books at the end of the volume.

Brumbaugh, Martin G. THE MAKING OF A TEACHER. New York: Harper and Brothers, 1905. Pp. xv 351. 2.00 (o.p.)

This volume on "making" as against "training" the teacher for work in Religious Education, would pass for *idealistic* today and suggest to many something of the impractical enthusiasm of the earlier generation. But the book is worth studying to balance the views now current which too often indicate an outlook entirely pragmatic and humanistic. Says the writer: "Teaching is always prophetic . . . It aims to equip the childhood of the present for the mature life that is to be . . . The Sunday School is not an organization primarily to acquaint children with biblical facts, but to set the currents of the soul in the channel of truth. . ." Some instructive and thought-provoking chapters have to do with "How Attention may be Secured," "Some Facts Concerning Memory," "The Building of Ideals," "The Use of Symbols," "Qualities that Make the Teacher a Good Governor," and "Educational Principles Used by Jesus."

Bryson, Lyman; Finkelstein, Louis; and others (editors): GOALS FOR AMERICAN EDUCATION, Ninth Symposium. New York: Harper and Brothers, (Distributors for the Conference on Science, Philosophy

and Religion in their Relation to the Democratic Way of Life, Inc.),
1950. Pp. xiv 555. 5.00

At this Ninth Conference, held in 1948, the main concern was,
"What Should be the Goals for Education?",—and of education set
above the secondary school level. Nineteen papers and comments by
prominent educators are represented in this volume, and in each
paper the place of Religion is either implied, discounted, or definitely
provided for. The commentators represent many and varied views—
Roman Catholic, Protestant, Jewish, Hindu (Swami Akhilananda),
naturalists and pragmatists. Thus, Robert Ulich presents a paper,
"On the Rise and Decline of Higher Education," T. V. Smith another
on "The Axiological Orientation of Higher Education", Louis A. J.
Mercier on "What Should be the Goals of Education Above the
Secondary School Level?" and Mordecai M. Kaplan one on "The Need
for Normative Unity in Higher Education." Especially provocative
of argument was the paper on "Education as Experiment" by President Harold Taylor of Sarah Lawrence College. A very lengthy and
exhaustive Index gives a good idea of the many subjects touched
upon incidentally during the course of the discussions.

Childs, John Lawrence. EDUCATION AND MORALS; An Experimentalist
Philosophy of Education. New York: Appleton-Century-Crofts, 1950.
Pp. xiv 299. 3.00

The subtitle of this text indicates both the character of the work
and the nature of the approach to the subject. Its emphasis is on moral
and religious values as these are discovered through experience. "No
school," says the writer, "would attempt to teach children to play
basketball, tennis, or any other game by simply having them read
books or listen to lectures by experts. Nor would we expect children
to learn how to behave in their relations with other human beings
apart from immediate experience with them." The text is mainly of
an essay character, in which the writer unfolds his reflections. Quotations are kept to a minimum; the emphasis is anti-traditionalist. "The
experimental mind believes that values evolve within the course of
ordinary experience. They have a natural basis and origin. . ."

Fitzpatrick, Edward Augustus. PHILOSOPHY OF EDUCATION. Milwaukee: Bruce Publishing Company, 1953. Pp. 477. 4.00

Fitzpatrick says that the book aims to do for religious humanism
what John Dewey's *Democracy and Education* did for a naturalistic
education. He accepts Dewey's statement that education is a reconstruction of experience, but insists that it is only then genuine education when it is used to achieve the highest mental, moral, and spiritual
potentiality of the individual. Man's powers—his urges, drives, emo-
tions, judgments, reasoning, and will—must be mastered so that he
may achieve his spiritual destiny.

Each chapter is prefaced with provocative questions and ends with
a Summary, some Propositions for Discussion, and a Bibliography.

Significant chapters are devoted to "The Nature of Man," "The Psychology of Education," and "Moral and Religious Education." Particularly interesting is the Glossary at the end of the book, which, along with definitions of terms and phrases used in Philosophy of Education, has a commentary enriched with quotations.

Greenstock, David Lionel. CHRISTOPHER TALKS TO CATHOLIC PARENTS. London: Burns and Oates, 1951. Pp. xiii 274. 18s

Here, and in a related series of books in which he identifies himself as "Christopher," Father Greenstock undertakes to interpret the principles of Christian education to parents and others entrusted with the care of souls. "The fundamental obligation of good Catholic parents," he says, "are to bring into the world and to educate, not merely good citizens of the civil state, but good citizens of the Kingdom of God, the Church." The most important thing in our life, he adds, is eternal salvation, which has to be won by our own efforts aided by the Grace of God. In the main, the book offers advice against the three evils of the world, the flesh and the devil. There are chapters on preparation for parenthood, the child's prayers, children and sex instruction, problems of adolescence, vocation and guidance, and "The Finished Product."

Kilpatrick, William H. PHILOSOPHY OF EDUCATION. New York: Macmillan Company, 1951. Pp. x 465. 5.00

Philosophy is defined by the author as "the critical study of the conflicting values of life to find out as best as possible how to manage life in the face of these conflicts." And Education is the "acting out of the best direction philosophizing can give." The approach to the subject is naturalistic and humanistic in the best tradition. Since man is an inseparable part of society, this book and philosophy of education orients man and his education in terms of his social environment, with the structure of the curriculum ordered according to this idea. A large part of the chapter on "The Life Good to Live" is given to Religion, which is defined as "the spirit with which one holds one's supreme value . . . plus the outworking of this attitude appropriately in life." Attention is also given to the contributions of modern Biology, Psychology, Sociology, and the scientific method in aiding man to appraise his own experience.

Lotz, Philip Henry, and Crawford, Leonidas Wakefield, (editors). STUDIES IN RELIGIOUS EDUCATION. Nashville, Tenn.: Cokesbury Press, 1931. Pp. 702. 3.50

Twenty-nine nationally known writers on the subject contribute chapters to this volume on Religious Education. Some significant chapters deal with the Development of Religious Education in America, the underlying Philosophy of Religious Education, Teaching Techniques, Tests and Measurements, Curriculum Content, the place of the Bible in Religious Education, Sunday and Week-Day Church

School, Character Education in Public Schools, and a very comprehensive Bibliography of Religious Education Books broken down according to subject matter divisions. Each chapter ends with suggestions for further study and a Bibliography.

The book should prove a gold mine of information on the subject, and a very detailed Index is a great help in tracing material. A noticeable lack is a chapter dealing with the early development of religious education as the idea sprang from the Synagogue schools and the Christian Catechetical schools.

Miller, Perry Gilbert E. and others. RELIGION AND FREEDOM OF THOUGHT. New York: Doubleday and Company, 1954. Pp. 64.

This collection of four essays on the theme "Religion and Freedom of Mind" represents the tribute of Union Theological Seminary to Columbia University at its bi-centennial celebration. Perry Miller writes on "The Location of American Religious Freedom," Robert L. Calhoun, on "The Historical Relations between Religion and Intellectual Freedom," Nathan L. Pusey on "Religion's Role in Education," and Reinhold Niebuhr on "The Commitment of the Self and Freedom of the Mind."

Tead, Ordway. CHARACTER BUILDING AND HIGHER EDUCATION. New York: Macmillan Company, 1953. Pp. 129. 2.00

Tead's address is the Kappa Delta Pi Lecture for 1953, and brings together his views on "character education." The author very definitely inveighs against the neutrality in matters of religion and morals which are usually expected of the teacher. "The truth would seem to me to be that, fully and properly within the law, our secular mandate may allow the teacher to read beyond the secular, a profoundly spiritual significance, into the facts of historical, natural-, and social-science findings, depending altogether upon his spiritual maturity, judgement, and taste." It is not enough that the college teach analysis of moral and religious problems, he stresses moral action. Of serious interest are his "Ten Commandments for All who Deal with College Students" (p. 61-2). Of prime importance, of course, is the material dealing with "The Influence of Religion" and the answers to such questions as "Is it essential that a student believe in God? Are there forces at work in the individual influencing against moral conduct? To what extent can education itself supply needed support to overcome human weakness? and What is the spiritual problem faced by "unchurched" young people?"

B. CHILDHOOD EDUCATION

AGREED SYLLABI ON RELIGIOUS INSTRUCTION FOR ENGLISH PUBLIC SCHOOLS

Section 26 of the Education Act of 1944 which was passed by Parliament, stated that religious instruction in English Public Schools must be in accordance with an "Agreed Syllabus" adopted for the school by the authorities concerned, and must not include any catechism or formulary distinctive of a particular religious denomination. These Syllabi stipulate the content of the course, in flexible outline form, from the Infant and Nursery state through the Secondary Schools.

AGREED SYLLABUS ON RELIGIOUS INSTRUCTION. England: County of Lincoln, 1951. Pp. 100.

Canon F. Hartford Cross, who writes an introduction to this Syllabus, points out that religious education is education both in theory and practice; that it is the substructure of all education in the broad sense, and that religious education brings light to the philosophy which is basic to the interplay of personalities. The material for the lower grades is the usual Bible content and familiarity. At the high school level (sixth form) this Syllabus has an interesting course on "Introduction to the Philosophy of Religion" which in American Colleges could be used for sophomores or juniors, and along with it another on "Christian Behavior."

AGREED SYLLABUS ON RELIGIOUS INSTRUCTION; Cheshire County. London: University of London Press, 1951.

The Agreed Syllabus for Cheshire County was prepared and agreed to by representatives of the Church of England, the Free Churches, and various educational committees. The program outlines cover Nursery class to the age of 18. The courses for various grades in the primary and secondary schools are informative and well filled in, and there is a good booklist at the end.

AGREED SYLLABUS ON RELIGIOUS INSTRUCTION. England: County of Yorkshire, 1947. Pp. vi 86.

Each of the Agreed Syllabi has varying degrees of merit, but each is scholarly and well organized, and reflects extensive and systematized instruction coming from a classical background. The foundations of this particular syllabus go back to 1904, and the present edition is a revision to suit current needs. For the older children there is a systematic study of the Gospels, an outline of Hebrew History, the idea of a "Church," Christian Ethics, the Philosophy of Religion, and the Relation between Religion and Science. Valuable and informative is a section initiating the student in a comparative study of the great religions of the world.

CAMBRIDGESHIRE SYLLABUS. Cambridge: Cambridge University Press, 1951. Pp. viii 184.

The Cambridgeshire Syllabus, as well as others, was agreed upon by representatives of the Church of England, the Free Churches, and educational authorities. It has a good introduction with an explanation of the issues involved, in Christian education. This text is also less out-line-like than some of the others, contains explanatory information for each graded lesson, and, at the end, an extensive list of books for reference and information on different subjects (covering pp. 157-82).

These additional Syllabi, which were not available for inspection and annotation, may also be of interest for either greater thorough-ness or a different point of view upon the subject matter.

AGREED SYLLABUS OF RELIGIOUS INSTRUCTION. Exeter, Eng-land: Exeter Educational Committee, City Education Offices, 1948. Pp. 40.

THE LONDON SYLLABUS OF RELIGIOUS EDUCATION. London: London County Council, The Council, 1947. Pp. 168.

AGREED SYLLABUS OF RELIGIOUS INSTRUCTION; Middlesex County. London: Middlesex County Council, 10 Great George Street, Westminister, 1948. Pp. 287.

SYLLABUS ON RELIGIOUS INSTRUCTION; Surrey County. Guilford, England: Biddles, Ltd., 1947. Pp. 110.

Cabot, Ella Lyman. ETHICS FOR CHILDREN; A Guide for Teachers and Parents. Boston, Houghton Mifflin Company, 1910. Pp. xxv 262. 2.00 (o.p.)

The inspiration for this book comes from a resolution of the Edu-cational Association of South Dakota which declared: "Whereas a sound morality is the very foundation of a truly progressive society and of a healthy public opinion, we recommend that systematic ethical in-struction be a part of a course of study in our public schools. We be-lieve that this instruction should be entirely divorced from partisan or sectarian bias and founded on a broad Christian basis." Cabot has put together material intended for children of six to fourteen years. The emphasis is not on moral lessons to reform bad traits, but the practice of ideals to help develop "unrealized goodness." Thus, each month of the year is singled out to realize, through example, story and precept, a particular virtue which young people admire. The grad-uated lessons of the chapters reflect fine psychological insight, and the book seems to be helpful without being "moralistic."

HUMAN VALUES IN THE ELEMENTARY SCHOOL. Washington, D. C.: National Education Association, Department of Elementary School Principals, 1952. Pp. 95. 1.00

The concern of this material is character education—how teaching and training in character should be made part of the elementary school curriculum. A section presents a gradation of the various values to be taught, with each one divided into its "conditions to be avoided" and "conditions to be sought." Chapters for Discussion involve exam-ination of such subjects as where human values come from, conditions making it difficult for a child to learn desired behavior, and others.

Outlined and with an evaluation are Study Units such as "Life in the Middle West," "The Arts—Appreciation and Expression," and "Science—An Outdoor Club." At the end of the major divisions of the booklet there are helpful bibliographies.

Fitch, Florence Mary. ONE GOD. New York: Lothrop, Lee and Shepard Company, 1944. Pp. xi 144.

For the student who wishes a quick look at the way Catholics, Jews, and Protestants worship, in general, this book can be a start. It is amply illustrated with pictures which supplement the printed material. In the section of the book entitled the Jewish Way these headings are the main ones: The Sabbath, Religion in the Home, Bar Mitzvah, The Synagogue, Conservative and Reform Jews, High Holy Days, Festivals, Hanukah, Passover.

In the Catholic Way these are the headings: Baptism, Home Training, The Church, Mass: The Holy Communion; Nuns and Monks, The First Communion, Confession, Confirmation and other Sacraments, Festivals of the Church, Easter, The World Wide Church.

In the section the Protestant Way these classifications are made: Variety in Protestant Churches, Baptism, The Protestant Home, The Church School, The Bible, The Services of Worship, Joining the Church, Festivals of the Church, The Friends.

Fitzpatrick, Edward Augustus, and Tanner, Paul F. METHODS OF TEACHING RELIGION IN ELEMENTARY SCHOOLS. Milwaukee: Bruce Publishing Company, 1939. Pp. viii 217. 2.75

The pedagogical philosophy of this book reflects the thesis that "the true Christian, the product of Christian education, is the supernatural man who thinks, judges, and acts constantly and consistently with right reason illumined by the supernatural light of the example and teaching of Christ." Character is understood as life dominated by principles, as distinguished from life dominated by mere impulses or external circumstances. The various chapters have to do with presenting "The Aim of Catholic Education," the role of "Knowledge in the Teaching of Religion," "Constructing the Curriculum," the various aids to be used and the various subjects to be taught. Among the chapters of general interest are those on "Religious Practices and Life" with its advice on such matters as Religion in Life, Training for the Virtuous Life, the "Psychology of Habit Formation" and "The Home in Religious Education."

Gilbert, Fred. TALKS TO CHILDREN. New York: Benziger Brothers, 1947. Pp. viii 203. 3.50

"The mysteries of religion are best communicated to the youthful mind through the mediums of a parable, an anecdote, an historical fact, or an incident of life," says the author. In this text the writer tries to translate the truths of the Christian religion into parables, anecdotes and living incidents. Thus, there are five chapters each dealing with the religious seasons, and others on The Sacraments, The Mass and Its Parts, as well as a series of "Talks on Timely Topics." The story of Barry, the heroic St. Bernard dog, who saved the lives of many, and who was killed when a traveler mistook the meaning of his help, is translated in terms of Divine purpose. Stories on plant and animal life are related to the ministry of Christ.

Hyde, William DeWitt. THE TEACHER'S PHILOSOPHY IN AND OUT OF SCHOOL. Boston: Houghton Mifflin Company, 1910. Pp. xiii 88. 1.25

In this monograph, President Hyde of Bowdoin College is concerned with the personality and character of the teacher. In the classroom as well as everywhere else, we must have *authority,* but is its seat to be vested in an official individual or in all individuals whose interests are involved? "Good teaching," says the author, "is simply democracy, Christianity, good-will, incarnate in the teacher, and diffused like an atmosphere throughout the school."

The book is divided into two parts, the first dealing with "The Teacher's Philosophy in School" and the second with "The Teacher's Philosophy out of School." There are five principles of personality which he emphasizes and which contribute to the make-up of the true teacher: Epicurean happiness (in the best sense), Stoical fortitude, Platonic serenity, Aristotelian proportion, and Christian devotion.

MacEachen, Roderick A. THE TEACHING OF RELIGION. New York: Macmillan Company, 1921. Pp. xi 240. 1.20 (o.p.)

The author "presents the truths of Faith in their true life setting." The teacher, he says, seeks "to enflame the hearts of the little ones with love for God and their fellow man . . . they learn to live in union with God, united with Him by the bonds of pure love." MacEachen writes from the view that "Religion is the bond of union between God and man" and that "religious teaching embraces the threefold sphere of knowledge, feeling, and conduct. It is intended to enable men to know, love, and serve God." The material is clearly and plainly presented, and is grounded on the philosophy that Religion is "a coordination of supernatural and human life." There are chapters on "The Meaning of the Religious Training," "The Content of the Teaching," "Character Building," "The Rule of Positives," the presentation of the various commandments, Divine Revelation, and the teaching and sacraments of the Church.

McDowell, John Bernard. THE DEVELOPMENT OF THE IDEA OF GOD IN THE CATHOLIC CHILD. Washington, D. C.: Catholic University Press, 1952. Pp. xiv 146. 1.75

Significant enough to be published, this dissertation involves an experimental test in three parts which includes a technical vocabulary, meanings, and descriptive terms for twelve of the attributes of God. It was administered to 2,263 boys and girls from the 4th through the 12th grade. The book will be useful to teachers of religion.

"Significant improvement appeared from the 4th through the 9th grade, after which little growth was apparent. The technical vocabulary used in the study was not understood by many; incorrect meanings were associated with many terms; there was evidence of memory without understanding and confusion caused by careless use of analogies. Older students tended to think of God as a spiritual Being, young children showed greater preference for the concrete and anthropomorphic expression. There was no evidence that these children put undue emphasis on fear of God. No stage of religious 'awakening' at any specific age was discovered; rather there was a continual improvement in understanding throughout most of the grades examined."

From the review by John L. Thomas, St. Louis University, in *Religious Education*, XLVIII (Nov.-Dec. 1953).

McLean, Angus Hector. THE IDEA OF GOD IN PROTESTANT RELIGIOUS EDUCATION. New York: Teachers College, Columbia University, (Contributions to Education, No. 410), 1930. Pp. 150. 1.50 (o.p.)

In this study there is an attempt to provide material to answer the questions,—What changes have occurred in the thinking of educated adults about God because of the scientific developments of recent years? and What changes have come about as the result of newer theological developments? Of course, the study confines itself to the idea of God in Protestant religious education as it is found in the elementary grades. No attempt was made to distinguish whether the conceptions of God varied with the different denominations, but the author assumed a general uniformity of view. There are informative chapters on "The Idea of God in Sunday School Teaching Materials" which show little variation and considerable uniformity, though drawn from different church backgrounds. Equally informative are the chapters on "What Do Children Think about God?" In the final chapter "How can Teaching about God be Improved?" Dr. MacLean offers two suggestions: "One of the outstanding needs is a revision of biblical teaching that will include more of the known facts of the Bible . . . Secondly, there is need for a similar advance in the teaching of the known facts of nature." There is added an excellent, though brief Bibliography of books.

Neumann, Henry. EDUCATION FOR MORAL GROWTH. New York: D. Appleton and Company, 1923. Unpaged. 2.50 (o.p.)

The author wrote from the standpoint of long experience as a teacher in Ethics and Education in the Ethical Culture School in New York City. The volume is addressed in general to teachers and those who have the obligation of developing the moral resources of the young. Its leanings are toward an experimental rather than dogmatic ethics, and for purposes of instruction the author makes a conscious effort to minimize appeals to authority. "Those who teach even the youngest need a plan of life for more than the single stage with which they deal," says the author, and he is intent on taking advantage of the period of life when moral idealism is at its best. Ethics, in this study, are related also to the principles of a democratic government. The book provides a background chapter explaining classical and modern systems of ethics.

REGULATIONS AND PROGRAMME FOR RELIGIOUS EDUCATION in the Public Schools. Ontario, Canada: Minister of Education, 1949. Pp. 70.

"The schools of Ontario," we are told, "exists for the purpose of preparing children to live in a democratic society which bases its way of life upon the Christian ideal . . . the school must seek to lead the child to choose and accept as his own those ideals of conduct and endeavor which a Christian and democratic society approves." The regulations provide allowing exemption from the exercises for any child whose parents or guardians request in writing that he is not to be compelled to participate.

In 1944, the regulations were revised to provide for religious teaching as part of the school program for Grades I to VI in the Ontario Public Schools.

The booklets for these grades are modifications of the "Agreed" Syllabi used in the various English countries. The manual of Regulations emphasizes that "the foundation of this course is the study of the Scriptures, which the teacher gives to Social Studies or to Science . . . Specific religious instruction, however, like any isolated and detailed knowledge, will be sterile and uninspiring goodness, beauty, and truth. Religious instruction must aim to set up ideals, Scriptural facts and Biblical texts."

The following books are listed as Teachers Guides to Religious Education. All of them may be obtained from the Ryerson Press, Toronto, Canada. The books form provision and experimental guides for the teachers. And they are urged to send criticism and comments about the books to the Minister of Education. The books are listed as guides to the individual teacher and should not take the place of individual study. (Listed by Grade)

Baker, Betty, and others. THE FRIEND OF LITTLE CHILDREN, Grade One. Toronto, Canada: Ryerson Press, 1954 (3rd printing) Pp. xiii 112. 1.00

Cox, Lilian E., and others. STORIES OF GOD AND JESUS, Grade Two. Toronto, Canada: Ryerson Press, 1955 (fourth printing). Pp. x 140. 1.00

Cox, Lilian E., and others. JESUS AND HIS FRIENDS, Grade Three. Toronto, Canada: Ryerson Press, 1955 (3rd printing). Pp. x 161. 1.00

Hayes, Ernest H., and Cox, Lilian. SERVANTS OF GOD, Grade Four. Toronto, Canada: Ryerson Press, 1955 (third printing). Pp. x 169. 1.00

Hayes, Ernest. LEADERS OF GOD'S PEOPLE, Grade Five. Toronto, Canada: Ryerson Press, 1955 (third printing). Pp. viii 181. 1.00

69

Hayes, Ernest, JESUS AND THE KINGDOM, Grade VI. Toronto, Canada: Ryerson Press, 1955 (third printing). Pp x 163. 1.00

Cox, Lillian, and Reed, Sidnell, and the editors. GOD AND MYSELF, LESSONS ON THE SECONDARY SECTIONS OF THE AGREED SYLLABUSES, Vol. I, Part I, Grade 7. Toronto, Canada: Ryerson Press, 1952 (fifth revised edition). Pp. 3 254. 1.50

Hayes, E. H., and Cox, L. E. MYSELF AND MY FELLOWS, Lessons on the Secondary Sections of the Agreed Syllabuses. Grade 8. Toronto, Canada: Ryerson Press, 1952. (4th revised edition). Pp. 3 320. 1.50

Tahon, Joseph V. THE FIRST INSTRUCTION OF CHILDREN AND BEGINNERS. St. Louis: B. Herder Book Company, 1930. Pp. 7 115. 1.25

In this brief history of the religious education of children, Father Tahon emphasizes that in the early centuries, instruction was carried out by the narrative rather than catechetical method. The writer is at pains to indicate the number of great teachers and Popes who endorsed this method against that of the straight rote memory of doctrine. He adds that in teaching them religion, children should be fed "milk" rather than "solid food." "Pedagogically, the best plan is to follow the steps of St. Augustine and to use the chronological order, neglecting, so to speak, during this period, the philosophical or theological order." An Appendix offers "Notes on the early Catechisms," such as those of Huss, Luther, St. Peter Canisius and the Westminster Shorter Catechism.

C. HIGH SCHOOL INSTRUCTION

Confrey, Burton. FAITH AND YOUTH; Experiences in the Religious Training of Catholic Youth as a Phase of Pastoral Theology. New York: Benziger Brothers, 1932. Pp. x 226. 2.00

This book "represents an effort to re-unite nature and grace in the hearts of young men, to master the eternal harmonies between the longings of the better self and the divine vision of life." As other volumes of the same type, this book is seriously conceived, does not approach religion or matters of faith argumentatively, and presumes the teachings of the Roman Catholic Church for a background. The various chapters deal with subjects which appeal to both youth of high school age and also early college—such as "Knights of Our Lady," "Preaching the Presence of God," and "Meditation and Spiritual Reading." An especially inviting aspect of the material is the frequent intrusion to the text of some student-written letter or some material with a personal or biographical touch.

Hennrich, Kilian Joseph. FORMING A CHRISTIAN MENTALITY; Chapters for the Religious Guidance of Youth, for Priests, Parents, and Teachers, New York: Joseph F. Wagner, Inc., 1946. Pp. xii 288. 2.75

Faith and *Worship* seem to be the natural divisions of the subject matter of this book. The method of exposition is catechetical in nature, and involves an extension of certain basic axioms. The sentences are for that reason terse and epigrammatic and need to be pondered upon. Under "Faith" are considered such subjects as "Christian Mentality," "Regeneration and Sanctification," and "Rearing Children in Faith and Piety." Under "Worship" is studied the liturgical life of the Church, and the knowledge and preparation for it. At the end, there is a selected Bibliography,—one part annotated, and the other a list of books from Roman Catholic sources. There is also a useful Glossary of the technical liturgical terms used in the text.

Hosty, Thomas J. STRAIGHT FROM THE SHOULDER. Milwaukee: Bruce Publishing Company, 1946. Pp. xiii 114. 2.25

These "Straight from the Shoulder" addresses were given to students at Retreats, and, as the Superintendent for the Archdiocese of Chicago says in the Preface, successfully by-pass "theological verbiage which is necessarily connected with the imparting of God's word." Here, in language the Roman Catholic youth of today can understand, he is told what he should be able to derive from the sermon, what is the purpose of his life on earth (as in ch. ii, "The Sixty-Four Dollar Question"), about telling lies, and other down-to-earth subjects. The last chapter is "A Postscript for Parents," and a reminder that whoever teaches another but does not himself live up to the teaching, can hardly expect to be heard.

Lord, Daniel Aloysius, S. J. SOME NOTES ON THE GUIDANCE OF YOUTH. St. Louis: Queen's Work, 1939. Pp. 11 174. 1.50

The title correctly describes the content of this little volume. It is a series of notes, in the form of anecdotes, stories from life, settings and conversations with and about youth, analyses of the views of those who work with them, and the philosophy underlying their guidance. Father Lord has been known especially for his frank and open way of writing about his subjects, and there is a charm about his practical and undogmatic simplicity. Here he considers those matters which constitute youth's moral and spiritual values: "False Guides," "Priests" and the way in which they fail in their obligation if they are not watchful, "Religious Teachers," "Attitude Toward Confidences," "Silence" and a host of other little subjects.

McGucken, William Joseph. S. J. THE JESUITS AND EDUCATION; The Society's Teaching and Practice, Especially in Secondary Education in the United States. Milwaukee: Bruce Publishing Company, 1932. Pp. xxv 352. 4.00 (o.p.)

The value of this volume lies in its presenting to the interested reader not only a perspective on Jesuit ideals of secondary education, but also a workable curriculum based on them. "The American Jesuit high school of the present day," says the author, "has been adapted to modern requirements along conservative lines, but American Jesuits have salvaged from the past a theory of education that is largely at variance with modern standards, a theory that mental discipline is a necessary factor in the training of the boy. This, partly, at least, explains their emphasis on the classics as a splendid instrument for intellectual development." He adds that the supreme objective since the days of St. Ignatius Loyola has been "the formation of the Christian citizen, obedient to the laws of God and the laws of the Church, obedient also to the laws of the State." Part I of the work treats of the origins of Jesuit instruction which resulted in the text called *Ratio Studiorum*. Part II deals with the Jesuit educational foundations in the U. S. Part III tells about the Jesuit high school, its curriculum, and the history of its development. Chapters especially fruitful for study are those dealing with "Objectives of Jesuit Teaching," "The High School Curriculum and Extra-Curricular Activities," and "The Jesuit Method of Instruction." There is an Appendix containing a translation of the *Ratio Studiorum* which is directly pertinent and which has Rules for the teacher and for the exposition of the subject matter. There is also a valuable 23-page descriptive Bibliography.

D. COLLEGES AND UNIVERSITIES

Bach, Marcus. OF FAITH AND LEARNING. Iowa City, Iowa: State University of Iowa, 1952. Pp. 250. 3.00

This publication commemorates the twenty-fifth anniversary of the School of Religion. The book is descriptive in nature of the backgrounds leading to the establishment of the school. It further relates how the school is administered and how the courses are taught.

Bell, Bernard Iddings. THE CRISIS IN EDUCATION. New York: Whittlesey House, 1949. Pp ix 237. 3.00

Bell's book is subtitled, "A Challenge to American Complacency." The book attempts to stir into action those who are complacent in American Education. Bell sees the student in modern education having much of his time wasted. One solution he proposes is a re-distribution of school time in order that talent not be wasted. Three chapters, 7, 8, and 9, seem very pertinent to the purposes of this bibliography. They are titled: "Experience and Education," "A Child's Religion," and "Religion and Higher Education."

COLLEGE READING AND RELIGION; A survey of college reading materials sponsored by the Edward W. Hazen Foundation and the Committee on Religion and Education of the American Council on Education. New Haven: Yale University Press, 1948. Pp. xi 345. 5.00

In this report, specialists from thirteen fields—History of Philosophy, Problems of Philosophy, Psychology, Psychiatry, History and Philosophy of Education, English Literature, Music, European History, Economics, Sociology, Cultural Anthropology, Physical Sciences, and Biological Sciences—survey the literature most commonly assigned for reading in their respective fields from the standpoint of the adequacy of the treatment of religion.

The chairman of the committee, Donald Cottrell, concluded from the study that religion is a neglected field of reading and study on the part of college students. He says, "The lightness of touch and even ignorance with which intellectual issues having a religious bearing or import are dealt with would seem little less than astonishing when the expansion of scholarship in general is taken into account . . . the hostility to religion revealed in some of the textbooks described becomes perhaps most effective when it is implied or suggested through the aggressive development of a positivistic attitude."

Collins, Joseph Burns. TEACHING RELIGION; AN INTRODUCTION TO CATECHETICS; A Text book for the Training of Teachers of Religion. Milwaukee: Bruce Publishing Company, 1953. Pp. 422. 4.00

"Religion involves the study of God and the things that pertain to the Creator and the Supreme Ruler; and it calls for a program of information and formation that will change the individual from a child of nature into a child of God. In the final analysis, a person's spiritual status will depend upon the quality and quantity of love that exist between him and his Creator . . .

As stated in the Introduction, the purpose of this book is not only to train future teachers of religion, but also to guide them in preparing student teachers. For that reason it is especially designed for teachers and directors of catechetical classes, high schools, colleges, seminaries, notivitates, and teacher institutes . . .

It is divided into four main parts, together with an Appendix . . . Part I is an outline of the history of Catechetics; Part II deals with the Principles and Methods of Teaching Religion; Part III has to do with Teaching Techniques; and in Part IV special methods and problems are handled."

From the review by Justin A. Driscoll, in *Religious Education,* XLIX (July-Aug. 1954)

Cunningham, William Francis. GENERAL EDUCATION AND THE LIBERAL COLLEGE. St. Louis: B. Herder Book Company, 1953. Pp. 286. 4.00

Father Cunningham seeks to redefine liberal education in terms of its goals, means, and methods. The three subdivisions of the work deal with the "Why," "What," and "How," of the process. The first section summarizes the Roman Catholic concept of the nature of education, and presents a threefold objective for liberal education; responsible leadership, intelligent followership, and co-operative fellowship.

In the longest portion, which examines the "What" or the curriculum, the author "Employing an ingenious wheel analogy distinguishes between hub, spoke, and rim subjects. The hub areas, including language, history, philosophy and theology (religion), are basic to all the others; breadth of education is the function of the spheral subjects, while the rim, or elective sources afford opportunities for depth of training. This is a lucidly organized and bluntly written book which contains a wealth of wisdom because it represents a fine synthesis of originality, insight, and experience in this field. Although presumably written for Catholic colleges, there is little in this book which does not apply equally well to institutions engaged in liberal education.

From the review by James J. Cribben, in *Religious Education,* XLIX (July-Aug. 1954)

Fairchild, Henry Pratt, (editor). THE OBLIGATION OF THE UNIVERSITIES TO THE SOCIAL ORDER; Addresses and Discussion at a Conference of Universities Under the Auspices of the New York University, 1932. New York: New York University Press, 1937. Pp. xlv 503. 3.00

On the occasion of the commemoration of the one-hundredth anniversary of New York University, a Conference was called which had for its theme, "The Obligation of the Universities to the Social Order." This volume brings together addresses from distinguished educators from all over the world. Section I contains addresses on the subject of "The University Today: Its Aims and Province"; Section II, "The University and Economic Changes"; Section III, "The University and Governmental Changes." To the reader interested in Religion in Education, Section IV is likely to be most serviceable. Under the title of "The University and Spiritual Values," there are six addresses and a series of discussions. Noteworthy among the addresses are W. E. Hocking's "Can Values be Taught," the poet, Alfred Noyes' "Aesthetic and Religious Values"; C. Nevil's "The Reality of Spiritual Values," and William Lewis' "Truth in Relation to Values." The volume in general reflects the philosophy and spirit of modern education and educational trends.

Fitzpatrick, Edward Augustus. EXPLORING A THEOLOGY OF EDUCATION. Milwaukee: Bruce Publishing Company, 1950. Pp. vii 174. 3.50

"Theology" of education is a relatively new field of exploration, but the writer says that it is an integral part of the Catholic philosophy of education. Where a "philosophy" of education often leads to scholarly looseness, a "theology" attempts to correct the indefiniteness of philosophy by relating the problem of the organization of knowledge to Revelation. "A philosophy of education can be organized just as in any other field, of knowledge. But a new element enters into a theology of education. It is faith. Unless there is faith that God revealed knowledge directly to mankind and that this revelation is known, then there can be no theology of education." The thesis is aptly developed in such chapters as "Some Major Doctrines and the Theology of Education," "Knowledge, Will and Love," and "Two Practical Issues: Religion in Public Education and Religion in Character Education."

Gauss, Christian Frederick (editor). THE TEACHING OF RELIGION IN HIGHER EDUCATION. New York: Ronald Press Company, 1951. Pp. viii 158. 2.75

The five chapters of the text are addressed to teachers and administrators who have the responsibility for developing courses in religion in higher education. The provision for the study and co-ordination of the reports was sponsored by The National Council on Religion in Higher Education and the Edward W. Hazen Foundation.

Dean Gauss contributes a chapter on "Religion and Higher Education in America," which deals with the historical background and brings the problem up to date. A chapter on "The Meaning of Liberal Education," is written by Prof. Robert Ulich who states that the underlying basis of liberal education must rest in the deeper faith that "human existence is imbedded in a transcendent reality . . ." which is the motivation and goal of man's intellectual, moral, and esthetic striving.

Pres. Howard B. Jefferson of Clark University describes "The Present Religious Situation in Higher Education." Chaplain Kenneth W. Morgan writes on "The Teaching of Religion in Higher Education," with sections on what a college graduate should know about religion, and courses in religion. The final chapter is the work of J. Hillis Miller, president of the University of Florida and deals with "Responsibility not Immunity"—indicating the issues involved in teaching religion in state universities, the need to challenge the secularization of life, and the religious program at the University of Florida.

Hartshorne, Hugh (editor). FROM SCHOOL TO COLLEGE. New Haven: Yale University Press, 1939. Pp. 446.

This study is concerned with what happened to 1200 boys who went from secondary school to college. It is concerned with their successes, failures, and problems. The study was conducted by Lincoln B. Hales, D. W. Bailey, and others. One hundred of the 1200 cases were studied intensively.

Hedley, George. RELIGION ON THE CAMPUS. New York: Macmillan Company, 1955. Pp. x 194. 2.75

Religion on the Campus is made up of a series of sermons given in the Chapel of Mills College. There are three sections to the book: (1) An Introductory for Freshman; (2) A Series about religion on the campus; (3) Sermons about student problems. In section two, can be found materials which are relevent for one who is seeking the relationship of religion to the fine arts, the natural sciences, and the humanities.

Limbert, Paul M. (editor). COLLEGE TEACHING AND CHRISTIAN VALUES. New York: Association Press, 1951. Pp. 187. 2.75

Limbert here writes the introductory and concluding chapters to explain and summarize the eight essays by prominent Christian laymen engaged in teaching the Physical Sciences, Biology, History, Economics, Sociology, Psychology, Literature and Religion. The essays are written with the conviction that college teaching is a "strategic front" in the struggle between Christianity and Secularism, and that a teacher who is also a Christian witness is a vital necessity. Thus, Kirtley F. Mather in the Physical Sciences, Douglas M. Knight in Literature, Eugene O. Golob in History, and William Spurrier in Religion are among the writers who tell of the manner in which their subjects can be used by a "witness for Christ." The editor contributes an initial "College Teaching as a Christian Vocation" and a closing "Basic Concerns and Contributions."

Livingstone, Richard Winn. SOME THOUGHTS ON UNIVERSITY EDUCATION. New York: Cambridge University Press, 1948. Pp. 29. 1.00

An eminent educator and former president of Corpus Christi College, Oxford, in this Fifth Annual Lecture of the National Book League, considers university education in terms of its present assets and future possibilities. He quotes Plato's statement that "the noblest of all studies is the study of what a man should be and how he should live," and enlarges upon it. Without imposing indoctrination, he would have some study of religion or philosophy or both be included in all undergraduate courses. In various of his works, he makes much of the thought of Bishop Berkeley: "Whatever the world thinks, he who hath not much meditated upon God, the human mind and the *Summum Bonum* may possibly make a thriving earthworm, but will certainly make a sorry patriot and a sorry statesman."

McMahon, John T. SOME METHODS OF TEACHING RELIGION. London: Burns Oates and Washburn, 1928. Pp. xiv 228.

This text is especially helpful in indicating the methods of imparting or eliciting knowledge from students, as the material grew out of the writer's own experience with the subject. Here is presented a description and an evaluation of the "Much Method," the "Yorke Method," "the Sower Scheme," "The Catechetical Method" and the "Shields Method." Part II is devoted to the "Project Principle of Teaching Religion." In this last the best aspects of the principles set down by John Dewey are utilized and made to bear fruit in religious education. In the latter portion of the book, the Project Method of Instruction is applied in detail in order to instruct children in the preparatory steps of the celebration of the Mass.

McKinney, Richard Ishmael. RELIGION IN HIGHER EDUCATION. AMONG NEGROES. New Haven: Yale University Press, 1945. Pp. xvi 165. 3.00

"The purpose of this investigation," says the author, "is to determine the present status of the religious policies and programs in the colleges for negroes, and to examine the significance of these for the negro student in view of the social setting of the education of this minority group." Sixteen schools were visited directly for this study, and consultations and questionnaires were used to procure data and information from thirty-three others. In the volume will be found a discussion of the attitudes of administrators, the status of religious workers, course offerings in Religion, the opinion of upper classmen on the religious life of the campus, and an analysis of general trends. The final chapter deals with "Findings and Recommendations," and there is an extensive Bibliography (books, periodicals and pamphlets) which brings together highly valuable information on the subject.

Morrison, Robert Bakewell (S.J.). CHARACTER FORMATION IN COL-LEGE. Milwaukee: Bruce Publishing Company, 1938. Pp. xiv 214. 1.85 (o.p.)

The author states he is transplanting the Aristotelian philosophy of conduct—that virtue makes a moral choice right—into terms which everyone can understand and put into practice. Revealed religion is deliberately kept in the background, and the subject-matter presented in words and arguments intelligible to the student and in such a manner as not to arouse the antagonism of anyone who does not pretend to any religion. Part I considers "Theory," and Part II has "Case Studies." The theory and the case studies are applied to such materials as "Character," "Resolutions," "Ideals," "Free Will," "Citizenship," and "Patriotism." The metaphysical foundations of the ethics discussed in the text are made explicit and summarized in the Appendix under "The Postulates."

Smith, Huston. THE PURPOSES OF HIGHER EDUCATION. New York: Harper and Brothers, 1955. Pp. xix 218. 3.50

Through a summation of the aims of higher education, which were reached through general faculty discussion, Huston Smith is able to bring these goals into focus. The book actually offers to the reader a statement on liberal education. It is concerned with the values with which higher education is concerned. The book is strengthened by quotations from various individuals such as these: Jacques Barzun, Nicholas Berdyaev, Fyodor Dostoeoski, Gilbert Highet, Jacques Maritain, Reinhold Niebuhr, Charles S. Peirce, St. Augustine, Harry Stack Sullivan, Arnold Toynbee, Paull Tillich, Alfred North Whitehead.

Walsh, Chad. CAMPUS GODS ON TRIAL. New York: Macmillan Company, 1953. Pp. 138. 2.75

There are really many gods on the campus, is Walsh's theme, and the real question for each student is, which god to follow. Some of the gods considered are Progress, Evolution, Humanitarianism, Americanism, and Communism. Every university professor will recognize the gods involved and what they stand for. The development of the argument paves the way for an exposition of the way to Christianity and the demands it makes of each one, "tough and tender, alluring and frightening, comforting and impossibly difficult." The style of the book, which should recommend it to students, is breezy and colloquial.

White, Lynn Townsend. EDUCATING OUR DAUGHTERS. New York: Harper and Brothers, 1950. Pp. x 166. 2.50

The intent of the book is religious, the language secular. The book is intended for parents concerned about the type of education their the student, too, who is thinking about his own educational develop-daughter should have. A very practical book which can be helpful for ment, Chapter 8, "Education for Catastrophe," is pertinent for the purposes of this bibliography.

RELIGION CONNECTED WITH THE STUDY OF MORAL AND SPIRITUAL VALUES

Brubacher, John Seiler (editor), and others. THE PUBLIC SCHOOLS AND SPIRITUAL VALUES. New York: Harper and Brothers, 1944. Pp. x 222. 2.50 (o.p.)

If our democracy is to prosper it must be in the quality of the people themselves. This is the thesis of this 7th yearbook of the John Dewey Society. The public school exists to nurture young people for an effective life and citizenship in a society. The "spiritual values" listed and which the school is to teach are: "moral right; integrity of thought and act; equal regard for human personality wherever found; faith in the free play of intelligence both to guide, study and to direct action; and, finally, those values of refined thought and feeling requisite to bring life to its finest quality."

The writers emphasize the historic separation of church and state and hold that these spiritual values can be taught without necessary recourse to religious authority and without reference to innate faculties. The essays are humanistic in inspiration and utilize the findings of the most recent social services.

Cabot, Ella Lyman. TEMPTATIONS TO RIGHT DOING. Boston: Houghton, Mifflin Company, 1929. Pp. xvii 311. 2.50 (o.p.)

Mrs. Cabot says that the aim of the books is "to bring together from actual experience the principle attractions to good living—in other words, the ideas, affections, interests and activities that make us prefer the right and reject the wrong. These magnets I call 'Temptations to Right-doing' in contrast with the better-known term, 'temptations to wrong-doing.' " "'Temptation" here is used in its wider meaning of incitement or attraction; temptations to right-doing are part of a moral tug of war and it is part of the teacher's problem to help the student himself pull in the right direction. The principal temptations to right-doing include: people, character training, interests, beauty, religion, and patriotism, "People we care about and who care for us are the first and greatest temptation to right-doing. The thought of them interpenetrates all the rest. We learn through a teacher fully as much as through his subject . . . The acceptance of responsibility is closely linked to the acceptance of our major human ties, and as for beauty and religion, they both haunt us with the longing for and thanksgiving to the other Self whom we recognize and seek and need to comprehend." Part I lists "Some Arch Tempters" (for right-doing), Part II has "Eight Ways of Becoming a Temptation," and Part IV lists "Powers not Ourselves" which help the soul to its end.

Finley, John Huston. THE MYSTERY OF THE MIND'S DESIRE. New York: Macmillan Company, 1936. Pp. viii 48. 1.00 (o.p.)

A notable educator extols, in this Kappa Delta Pi Lecture, "the mystery of an urge that will not let man rest satisfied with what he was or is, however much he may respect the sanctions of the past or be tempted to inertness by the comforts of the present,—the desire for knowledge, the desire to know the utmost truth, which has its highest expression in beauty." The address rises to heights of poetic grandeur, and presents spiritual culture in a light not usual for such occasions. He says on one page, "To be seeing the world made new every morning, as if it were the morning of the first day, and then to make the most of it for the individual soul as if it were the last day—is the daily curriculum of the mind's desire."

Healy, Edwin F., S.J. MORAL GUIDANCE. Chicago: Loyola University Press, 1942. Pp. xii 351. 2.00

Moral Guidance was written as an intended help to better understanding of the Christian principles of morality, and also as a help to Catholic laymen to understand the true and unchanging doctrines of moral conduct. The book is written in a very forthright manner and states its propositions in very simple language. The purpose behind the study of Moral Guidance, says the author, is to confront and to solve the ordinary religious difficulties which arise in every Christian's life. The study makes "full use" (the author's words) of divine revelation. After explaining moral guidance and some principles of ethics, the writer devotes individual chapters to the ten commandments. Especially useful and practical are the chapters on the duties of judges, lawyers, doctors, nurses, business men, and public officials. Appended to each chapter there are Topics for Discussion and Cases to be Analyzed.

Hyde, William DeWitt. THE QUEST OF THE BEST. Insights into Ethics for Parents, Teachers, and Leaders of Boys. New York: Thos. Y. Crowell Company, 1913. Pp. vi 267. (o.p.)

Much good advice is to be found in the easily read pages of this book. Writes President Hyde of Bowdoin College: "The Quest for the Best is the aim to fulfill each interest so far as it furthers the fulfillment, in proportion of their worth and claim, of all interests of all persons. It aims to conserve the good latent in natural badness and to avoid the badness inseparable from artificial goodness. It is therefore extremely difficult and never completely attained . . ." He adds that in putting this material together, he has drawn as much from Plato and Aristotle as from Jesus and Paul. He confines himself to ethics and steers clear of theology. And we are told that the Quest for the Best for self, for others and for society, is another name for Jesus' word *love,* but without the sentimental associations which have grown around the word. The titles of some of the chapters give a good picture of the development of the book: "Natural Badness and the Germ of Goodness"; "Artificial Goodness the Repression of Badness"; "The Quest of the Best," and "Missing the Best: Sins of Excess and Defect."

Livingstone, Richard Winn. ON EDUCATION; The Future in Education and Education for a World Adrift. London: Combridge University Press, 1954. Pp. 231. 3.00

Two books, originally published separately, are brought together into one volume. *Education for a World Adrift,* the writer tells us, is an attempt to consider what Education can do to remedy the lack of standards and clear beliefs which is the most dangerous weakness of the Western world. *The Future in Education* was the fruit of reflection on the results of our present educational system. Sir Richard's work is philosophical and thought-provoking. "It is not a question of what the ordinary boy or girl knows or does not know, when they leave school; it is a question of the interests and tastes which they carry with them into life." In an indirect way, the author pleads for greater emphasis on Adult Education and for an education that affects character.

MORAL AND SPIRITUAL VALUES IN THE PUBLIC SCHOOLS. Washington, D. C.: Education Policies Commission, NEA, 1951. Pp. xi 100.

The keynote of this statement of perspective is "That which out of their intelligence and experience the people declare to be good, they will attempt to maintain and perpetuate." The "values" considered desirable for perpetuation, are those generally agreed upon, such as the value of human personality, moral responsibility, respect for excellence, moral equality, and others. Very thought-provoking is the moral situation involved in Johnny's receiving from a storekeeper a dime in mistake for a penny. Various solutions, legal, moral, social, and authoritarian, are considered. While the view of the booklet favors no particular religious outlook, its approach to the subject of teaching moral and spiritual values is humanistic and practical.

Yeaxlee, Basil Alfred. SPIRITUAL VALUES IN ADULT EDUCATION, A Study of a Neglected Aspect. New York: Oxford University Press, 1925 (two volumes). Pp. 318; 455. 8.75 (o.p.)

The material in these two volumes was approved for the Ph.D. degree at the University of London, and represents something of a pioneer effort, not only to organize the subject, but also to give it pointed application. There are well-documented chapters on such matters as Education as a Spiritual Activity, the Relation of Adult Education to Religion, Adult Education in the Churches, and a consideration of the general forces which brought out the need for relating Education and Religion into the open. The second volume has an instructive section on "A Detailed Survey of Adult Education Activities in Churches and Kindred Organizations."

INDEX

SECTION I

GENERAL PROBLEMS OF RELIGION IN EDUCATION

Allen, Henry Elisha	RELIGION IN THE STATE UNIVERSITY	1
Blau, Joseph Leon (editor)	CORNERSTONES OF RELIGIOUS FREEDOM IN AMER-ICA	1
Bower, William Clayton M.	MORAL AND SPIRITUAL VALUES IN EDUCATION ..	1
Bryson, Lyman (editor)	FREEDOM AND AUTHORITY IN OUR TIME	2
Butts, Robert Freeman	AMERICAN TRADITION IN RELIGION AND EDU-CATION	2
Fleming, William Sherman	GOD IN OUR PUBLIC SCHOOLS	3
Hay, Clyde Lemont	THE BLIND SPOT IN AMERICAN PUBLIC EDUCA-TION	3
Hullfish, Henry Gordon (editor)	EDUCATIONAL FREEDOM IN AN AGE OF ANXIETY	3
Johnson, Alvin Walter & Yost, Frank H.	SEPARATION OF CHURCH AND STATE IN THE UNITED STATES	4
Johnson, Frederick Ernest (editor)	AMERICAN EDUCATION AND RELIGION	4
Lippman, Walter	AMERICAN INQUISITORS	5
McCollum, Vashti Cromwell	ONE WOMAN'S FIGHT	5
Martin, Renwick Harper	OUR PUBLIC SCHOOLS, CHRISTIAN OR SECULAR ..	5
Nelson, Claud D.	CHURCH AND STATE	6
Niebuhr, Richard H.	CHRIST AND CULTURE	6
O'Neill, James Milton	RELIGION AND EDUCATION UNDER THE CON-STITUTION	6
—————————	CATHOLICISM AND AMERICAN FREEDOM	7
Pfeffer, Leo	CHURCH, STATE, AND FREEDOM	7
Stokes, Anson Phelps	CHURCH AND STATE IN THE UNITED STATES	8
Thayer, Vivian Trow	ATTACK UPON THE AMERICAN SECULAR SCHOOL	8
Wroten, James D.	EXPERIMENTAL DEVELOPMENT OF A COLLEGE COURSE IN CHURCH AND SOCIETY	8
Yale University Divinity School	RELIGION IN STATE TEACHERS COLLEGES	9

SECTION II

CLARIFICATION OF THE SUBJECT

Bower, William Clayton	CHURCH AND STATE IN EDUCATION	10
Brinton, Howard Haines	QUAKER EDUCATION IN THEORY AND PRACTICE ..	10
Brown, Kenneth Irving	NOT MINDS ALONE	10
Brubacher, John Seiler	MODERN PHILOSOPHIES OF EDUCATION	11
Butterfield, Herbert	CHRISTIANITY AND HISTORY	11
Connell, Francis Jeremiah	MORALS IN POLITICS AND PROFESSIONS	11
Cunningham, William Francis	THE PIVOTAL PROBLEMS OF EDUCATION	11
Dawson, Joseph M.	AMERICA'S WAY IN CHURCH, STATE AND SOCIETY	12
Dracher, Norman M.	INFLUENCE OF SECTARIANISM, NON-SECTARIANISM, AND SECULARISM UPON THE PUBLIC SCHOOLS OF DETROIT AND THE UNIVERSITY OF MICHI-GAN, 1837-1900	12
Encyclical Letter of Pope Pius XI	ON THE CHRISTIAN EDUCATION OF YOUTH	12
Fairchild, Hoxie Neale (editor)	RELIGIOUS PERSPECTIVES IN COLLEGE TEACHING	13

Ferre, Nels Frederick S.	CHRISTIAN FAITH AND HIGHER EDUCATION	13
	FUNCTION OF THE PUBLIC SCHOOLS IN DEALING WITH RELIGION	13
Gaebelein, Frank Ely	CHRISTIAN EDUCATION IN A DEMOCRACY	14
Ginzberg, Eli	AGENDA FOR AMERICAN JEWS	14
Hedley, George Percy	SUPERSTITIONS OF THE IRRELIGIOUS	14
Henry, Nelson B. (editor)	MODERN PHILOSOPHIES AND EDUCATION	15
Henry, Virgil	PLACE OF RELIGION IN THE PUBLIC SCHOOLS	15
Hudson, Winthrop Still	GREAT TRADITION OF THE AMERICAN CHURCHES	15
Keller, James Gregory	ALL GOD'S CHILDREN	16
Kirsch, Felix M.	RELIGIOUS TEACHER'S LIBRARY	16
Lowry, Howard	MIND'S ADVENTURE	17
Madden, Ward Ellis	RELIGIOUS VALUES IN EDUCATION	17
Moberly, Walter Hamilton	CRISIS IN THE UNIVERSITY	17
Murray, Albert Victor	EDUCATION INTO RELIGION	18
Neumann, Henry	LIVES IN THE MAKING	18
O'Leary, Mary Florence M.	CATHOLIC CHURCH AND EDUCATION	19
Ortega y Gassett, José	MISSION OF THE UNIVERSITY	19
Painter, Franklin V. N.	LUTHER ON EDUCATION	19
Redden, John D., and Ryan, Francis A.	FREEDOM THROUGH EDUCATION	20
Religion and Education of A C E Series	RELATION OF RELIGION TO PUBLIC EDUCATION; BASIC PRINCIPLES	20
Van Dusen, Henry Pitney	GOD IN EDUCATION, A TRACT FOR THE TIMES	20
Wilder, Amos N. (editor)	LIBERAL LEARNING IN RELIGION; A VITAL DISCUSSION OF MAJOR ISSUES	21
Wilson, Karl K.	HISTORICAL SURVEY OF RELIGIOUS CONTENT OF AMERICAN GEOGRAPHY TEXTBOOKS FROM 1784 TO 1895	21

SECTION III

RELIGION IN THE HUMANITIES

III. A. PHILOSOPHY

Bennett, Charles Andrew A.	DILEMMA OF RELIGIOUS KNOWLEDGE	22
Berkson, Isaac Baer	EDUCATION FACES THE FUTURE	22
Burtt, Edwin Arthur	TYPES OF RELIGIOUS PHILOSOPHY	23
Butler, James Donald	FOUR PHILOSOPHIES AND THEIR PRACTICE IN EDUCATION AND RELIGION	23
Cabot, Richard Clarke	MEANING OF RIGHT AND WRONG	24
Conger, George Perrigo	IDEOLOGIES OF RELIGION	24
Connell, Francis Jeremiah	OUTLINES OF MORAL THEOLOGY	24
Davidson, Robert Franklin	PHILOSOPHIES MEN LIVE BY	25
Dewey, John	A COMMON FAITH	25
Everett, Millard Spencer	IDEALS OF LIFE	25
Hartshorne, Charles, and Reese, William L.	PHILOSOPHERS SPEAK OF GOD	26
Huxley, Aldous Leonard	PERENNIAL PHILOSOPHY	26
Hyde, William DeWitt	FIVE GREAT PHILOSOPHIES OF LIFE	27
Kallen, Horace Meyer	EDUCATION OF FREE MEN	27
Robinson, Daniel Sommer	PRINCIPLES OF CONDUCT	27
Sayers, Ephraim Vern	FIRST COURSE IN PHILOSOPHY OF EDUCATION	28
Spann, John Richard (editor)	CHURCH AND SOCIAL RESPONSIBILITY	28
Stace, Walter Terence	CONCEPT OF MORALS	29
Wieman, Henry Nelson, and Meland, Bernard E.	AMERICAN PHILOSOPHIES OF RELIGION	29

III. B. PSYCHOLOGY

Adler, Alfred	UNDERSTANDING HUMAN NATURE	30
Allan, Denison Maurice	REALM OF PERSONALITY	30

Allport, Gordon W.   INDIVIDUAL AND HIS RELIGION 30
————————   BECOMING 31
Dreikurs, Rudolph   CHARACTER EDUCATION AND SPIRITUAL VALUES
     IN AN ANXIOUS AGE 31
Fromm, Erich   MAN FOR HIMSELF 31
Hollingworth, Harry L.   PSYCHOLOGY AND ETHICS 32
James, William   TALKS TO TEACHERS, AND TO STUDENTS ON SOME
     OF LIFE'S IDEALS 32
Jung, Carl Gustav   MODERN MAN IN SEARCH OF A SOUL 33
King, William Peter (editor)   BEHAVIORISM; A BATTLE LINE 33
Ligon, Ernest Mayfield   A GREATER GENERATION 33
Link, Henry Charles   RETURN TO RELIGION 34
McDougall, William   CHARACTER AND THE CONDUCT OF LIFE 34
————————   FRONTIERS OF PSYCHOLOGY 34
May, Rollo   MAN'S SEARCH FOR HIMSELF 35
Scheidlinger, Saul   PSYCHOANALYSIS AND GROUP BEHAVIOR 35

III. C. THE STUDY OF LITERATURE AS A RECORD OF LIFE

Baldwin, Robert Chester and   AN INTRODUCTION TO PHILOSOPHY THROUGH
     McPeek, James A. S.   LITERATURE 35
Demiashkevich, Michael John   NATIONAL MIND, ENGLISH-FRENCH-GERMAN 36
Jones, Howard Mumford   IDEAS IN AMERICA 36
————————   THEORY OF AMERICAN LITERATURE 37
Miller, Perry Gilbert E.   NEW ENGLAND MIND 37
Scheele, Sister M. Augustine   EDUCATIONAL ASPECTS OF SPIRITUAL WRITING... 38
Weatherhead, Leslie Dixon   PSYCHOLOGY IN THE SERVICE OF THE SOUL 38

SECTION IV

RELIGION IN THE SOCIAL SCIENCES

IV. A. ECONOMICS

Baum, Maurice (compiler)   READINGS IN BUSINESS ETHICS, A SURVEY OF THE
     PRINCIPLES AND PROBLEMS OF AMERICAN
     BUSINESS MORALITY 39
Bennett, John Coleman   CHRISTIAN VALUES AND ECONOMIC LIFE 39
Boulding, Kenneth E.   ORGANIZATIONAL REVOLUTION, A STUDY IN THE
     ETHICS OF ECONOMIC ORGANIZATION 40
Bowen, Howard Rothmann   SOCIAL RESPONSIBILITIES OF THE BUSINESS MAN 40
Childs, Marquis William, and   ETHICS IN A BUSINESS SOCIETY 40
     Cater, Douglass
Demant, Vigo Auguste   RELIGION AND THE DECLINE OF CAPITALISM 41
Hoyt, Elizabeth Ellis   AMERICAN INCOME AND ITS USE 41
Ryan, John Augustine   A LIVING WAGE, ITS ETHICAL AND ECONOMIC
     ASPECTS 41
Stamp, Josiah Charles   CHRISTIANITY AND ECONOMICS 42
Tawney, Richard Henry   RELIGION AND THE RISE OF CAPITALISM, A HIS-
     TORICAL STUDY 42
Ward, Alfred Dudley   GOALS OF ECONOMIC LIFE 43
————————   AMERICAN ECONOMY—ATTITUDES AND OPINIONS 43
Ward, Harry Frederick   OUR ECONOMIC MORALITY AND THE ETHICS OF
     JESUS 43

IV. B. HISTORY AND HISTORICAL PERSPECTIVES

Greene, Evarts B.   RELIGION AND THE STATE, THE MAKING AND TEST-
     ING OF AN AMERICAN TRADITION 44
Hallowell, John Hamilton   MAIN CURRENTS IN MODERN POLITICAL THOUGHT 44
————————   MORAL FOUNDATIONS OF DEMOCRACY 44
Niebuhr, Reinhold   FAITH AND HISTORY 44
Shinn, Roger L.   CHRISTIANITY AND THE PROBLEM OF HISTORY .. 45
Toynbee, Arnold Joseph   A STUDY OF HISTORY; AN ABRIDGMENT OF
     VOLUMES I-VI, BY D. C. SOMERVILL 45

IV. C. POLITICAL SCIENCE AND GOVERNMENT

Callender, Clarence N., and Charlesworth, James C. (editors) — ETHICAL STANDARDS IN AMERICAN PUBLIC LIFE — 45

Chandler, Albert Richard — THE CLASH OF POLITICAL IDEALS — 46

Douglass, Paul Howard — ETHICS IN GOVERNMENT — 46

Ebersole, Luke Eugene — CHURCH LOBBYING IN THE NATION'S CAPITAL — 46

Gerhart, Eugene C. — AMERICAN LIBERTY AND "NATURAL LAW" — 47

Hyma, Albert — CHRISTIANITY AND POLITICS — 47

Keller, James Gregory — YOU CAN CHANGE THE WORLD — 48

MacIver, Robert Morrison (editor) — CONFLICT OF LOYALTIES — 48

Osgniach, Augustine John — CHRISTIAN STATE — 48

Rogers, Edward — A CHRISTIAN COMMENTARY ON COMMUNISM — 49

IV. D. SOCIOLOGY AND SOCIAL MOVEMENTS

Casserley, Julien Victor L. — MORALS AND MAN IN THE SOCIAL SCIENCES — 49

Cook, Lloyd Allen, and Cook, Elaine F. — INTERGROUP EDUCATION — 50

Hughley, Judge Neal — TRENDS IN PROTESTANT SOCIAL IDEALISM — 50

Hutchison, John Alexander (editor) — CHRISTIAN FAITH AND SOCIAL ACTION — 50

May, Henry Farnham — PROTESTANT CHURCHES AND INDUSTRIAL AMERICA — 51

Neill, Thomas Patrick — RELIGION AND CULTURE; THE CHRISTIAN IDEA OF MAN IN CONTEMPORARY SOCIETY — 51

Niebuhr, Reinhold — DOES CIVILIZATION NEED RELIGION? — 51

Nottingham, Elizabeth Kristine — RELIGION AND SOCIETY — 52

Sherrington, Charles Scott — MAN ON HIS NATURE — 52

Sweet, William Warren — RELIGION IN THE DEVELOPMENT OF THE AMERICAN CULTURE, 1765-1840 — 53

Troeltsch, Ernst — THE SOCIAL TEACHINGS OF THE CHRISTIAN CHURCHES — 53

SECTION V

RELIGION IN THE NATURAL SCIENCES

V. A. THE PHILOSOPHY OF SCIENCE

Barnes, Ernest William — SCIENTIFIC THEORY AND RELIGION, THE WORLD DESCRIBED BY SCIENCE AND ITS SPRITUAL INTERPRETATION — 54

Eddington, Arthur Stanley — SCIENCE AND THE UNSEEN WORLD — 54

Heim, Karl — TRANSFORMATION OF THE SCIENTIFIC WORLD VIEW — 55

Hocking, William Ernest — SCIENCE AND THE IDEA OF GOD — 55

Russell, Bertrand — RELIGION AND SCIENCE — 56

V. B. CHEMISTRY AND PHYSICS

Whitehead, Alfred North — CONCEPT OF NATURE, LECTURES DELIVERED IN TRINITY COLLEGE — 56

V. C. CONNECTED WITH VARIOUS ASPECTS OF MATHEMATICS

Coulson, Charles Alfred — SCIENCE AND CHRISTIAN BELIEF — 56

Whitehead, Alfred North — ESSAYS IN SCIENCE AND PHILOSOPHY — 57

V. D. BIOLOGY AND ZOOLOGY

Drummond, Henry — NATURAL LAW IN THE SPIRITUAL WORLD — 57

DuNoüy, Pierre Lecomte — HUMAN DESTINY — 57

Haldane, John Scott — SCIENCES AND PHILOSOPHY — 58

Mason, Frances Baker (editor) CREATION BY EVOLUTION 58
Sinnott, Edmund Ware CELL AND PSYCHE, THE BIOLOGY OF PURPOSE ... 59
————————— TWO ROADS TO TRUTH 59
————————— BIOLOGY OF THE SPIRIT 59

SECTION VI

RELIGION IN PROFESSIONAL EDUCATION

VI. A. THE PRINCIPLES OF EDUCATION

Agnesine, Sister M. TEACHING RELIGION FOR LIVING 60
Brumbaugh, Martin G. MAKING OF A TEACHER 60
Bryson, Lyman; Finkelstein, Louis, and others (editors) GOALS FOR AMERICAN EDUCATION, NINTH SYMPOSIUM 60
Childs, John Lawrence EDUCATION AND MORALS, AN EXPERIMENTALIST PHILOSOPHY OF EDUCATION 61
Fitzpatrick, Edward Augustus PHILOSOPHY OF EDUCATION 61
Greenstock, David Lionel CHRISTOPHER TALKS TO CATHOLIC PARENTS 62
Kilpatrick, William H. PHILOSOPHY OF EDUCATION 62
Lotz, Philip Henry and Crawford, Leonidas W. (editors) STUDIES IN RELIGIOUS EDUCATION 62
Miller, Perry Gilbert E., and others RELIGION AND FREEDOM OF THOUGHT 63
Tead, Ordway CHARACTER BUILDING AND HIGHER EDUCATION.. 63

VI. B. CHILDHOOD EDUCATION

Agreed Syllabi on Religious Instruction for English Schools AGREED SYLLABUS ON RELIGIOUS INSTRUCTION, County of Lincoln 64

————————— —————————, Cheshire County 64

————————— —————————, County of Yorkshire 64
————————— CAMBRIDGE SYLLABUS, Cambridge 64
————————— AGREED SYLLABUS ON RELIGIOUS INSTRUCTION, Exeter 65
————————— THE LONDON SYLLABUS OF RELIGIOUS INSTRUCTION 65
————————— THE AGREED SYLLABUS OF RELIGIOUS EDUCATION, Middlesex County 65
————————— SYLLABUS ON RELIGIOUS INSTRUCTION, Surrey County 65
Cabot, Ella Lyman ETHICS FOR CHILDREN, A GUIDE FOR TEACHERS AND PARENTS 65
Elementary School Principals (NEA) HUMAN VALUES IN THE ELEMENTARY SCHOOL.. 65
Fitch, Florence Mary ONE GOD 66
Fitzpatrick, Edward A. and Tanner, Paul F. METHODS OF TEACHING RELIGION IN ELEMENTARY SCHOOLS 66
Gilbert, Fred TALKS TO CHILDREN 66
Hyde, William DeWitt TEACHER'S PHILOSOPHY IN AND OUT OF SCHOOL 67
MacEachen, Roderick A. TEACHING OF RELIGION 67
McDowell, John Bernard DEVELOPMENT OF THE IDEA OF GOD IN THE CATHOLIC CHILD 67
McLean, Angus Hector IDEA OF GOD IN PROTESTANT RELIGIOUS EDUCATION 68
Neumann, Henry EDUCATION FOR MORAL GROWTH 68
REGULATIONS AND PROGRAMME FOR RELIGIOUS EDUCATION, in Public Schools of Ontario, Canada 69

VI. B. CHILDHOOD EDUCATION (continued)

Baker, Betty, and others — FRIEND OF LITTLE CHILDREN, Grade One 69

Cox, Lilian E. and others — STORIES OF GOD AND JESUS, Grade Two 69

———— — JESUS AND HIS FRIENDS, Grade Three 69

Hayes, Ernest H. and Cox, Lilian E. — SERVANTS OF GOD, Grade Four 69

Hayes, Ernest H. — LEADERS OF GOD'S PEOPLE, Grade Five 69

———— — JESUS AND THE KINGDOM, Grade Six 70

Cox, Lillian E. and Reed, Sidnell, and the editors — GOD AND MYSELF, LESSONS ON THE SECONDARY SECTIONS OF THE AGREED SYLLABUSES, Grade Seven 70

Hayes, Ernest H., and Cox, Lilian E. — MYSELF AND MY FELLOWS, LESSONS IN THE SECONDARY SECTIONS OF THE AGREED SYLLABUSES, Grade Eight 70

Tahon, Joseph V. — FIRST INSTRUCTION OF CHILDREN AND BEGINNERS 70

VI. C. HIGH SCHOOL INSTRUCTION

Confrey, Burton — FAITH AND YOUTH, EXPERIENCES IN THE RELIGIOUS TRAINING OF CATHOLIC YOUTH AS A PHASE OF PASTORAL THEOLOGY 70

Hennrich, Killan J. — FORMING A CHRISTIAN MENTALITY, CHAPTERS FOR RELIGIOUS GUIDANCE OF YOUTH, FOR PRIESTS, PARENTS, AND TEACHERS 70

Hosty, Thomas J. — STRAIGHT FROM THE SHOULDER 71

Lord, Daniel A. (S.J.) — SOME NOTES ON THE GUIDANCE OF YOUTH 71

McGucken, William J. (S.J.) — JESUITS AND EDUCATION, THE SOCIETY'S TEACHING AND PRACTICE, ESPECIALLY IN SECONDARY EDUCATION IN THE UNITED STATES 71

VI. D. COLLEGES AND UNIVERSITIES

Bach, Marcus Louis — OF FAITH AND LEARNING 72

Bell, Bernard Iddings — CRISIS IN EDUCATION 72

— COLLEGE READINGS AND RELIGION 72

Collins, Joseph Burns — TEACHING RELIGION; AN INTRODUCTION TO CATECHETICS 73

Cunningham, William Francis — GENERAL EDUCATION AND THE LIBERAL COLLEGE.. 73

Fairchild, Henry Pratt (editor) — THE OBLIGATIONS OF THE UNIVERSITY TO THE SOCIAL ORDER 74

Fitzpatrick, Edward Augustus — EXPLORING A THEOLOGY OF EDUCATION 74

Gauss, Christian Frederick (editor) — TEACHING OF RELIGION IN HIGHER EDUCATION.. 74

Hartshorne, Hugh (editor) — FROM SCHOOL TO COLLEGE 75

Hedley, George — RELIGION ON THE CAMPUS 75

Limbert, Paul M. (editor) — COLLEGE TEACHING AND CHRISTIAN VALUES .. 75

Livingstone, Richard Winn — SOME THOUGHTS ON UNIVERSITY EDUCATION .. 76

McMahon, John T. — SOME METHODS OF TEACHING RELIGION 76

McKinney, Richard I. — RELIGION IN HIGHER EDUCATION AMONG NEGROES 76

Morrison, Robert Bakewell (S.J.) — CHARACTER FORMATION IN COLLEGE 77

Smith, Huston — PURPOSES OF HIGHER EDUCATION 77

Walsh, Chad — CAMPUS GODS ON TRIAL 77

White, Lynn Townsend — EDUCATING OUR DAUGHTERS 77

VII. RELIGION CONNECTED WITH THE STUDY OF MORAL AND SPIRITUAL VALUES

Brubacher, John Sciler (editor), and others — PUBLIC SCHOOLS AND SPIRITUAL VALUES 79

Cabot, Ella Lyman — TEMPTATIONS TO RIGHT DOING 79

Finley, John Huston — MYSTERY OF THE MIND'S DESIRE 80

Healy, Edwin F. (S.J.)   MORAL GUIDANCE 80
Hyde, William DeWitt   QUEST OF THE BEST. INSIGHT INTO ETHICS 80
Livingstone, Richard Winn   ON EDUCATION 81
Education Policies Commission   MORAL AND SPIRITUAL VALUES IN THE PUBLIC
   SCHOOLS 81
Yeaxlee, Basil Alfred   SPIRITUAL VALUES AND ADULT EDUCATION 81

AUTHORS' INDEX

Adler, Alfred 30
Agnesine, Sister M. 60
Allan, Denison Maurice 30
Allen, Henry Elisha 1
Allport, Gordon W. 30, 31
American Council on Education . 20

Bach, Marcus Louis 72
Bainton, Ronald H. ....
Baker, Betty 69
Baldwin, Robert Chester 35
Barnes, Ernest William 54
Baum, Maurice 39
Bell, Bernard Iddings 72
Bennett, Charles Andrew 22
Bennett, John Coleman 39
Berkson, Isaac Baer 22
Blau, Joseph Leon 1
Boulding, Kenneth E. 40
Bowen, Howard Rothmann 40
Bower, William Clayton 1, 10
Brinton, Howard Haines 10
Brown, Kenneth Irving 10
Bryson, Lyman 2, 60
Brubacher, John Seiler 11, 79
Brumbaugh, Martin G. 60
Burtt, Edwin Arthur 23
Butler, James Donald 23
Butts, Robert Freeman 2
Butterfield, Herbert 11

Cabot, Ella Lyman 65, 79
Cabot, Richard Clarke 24
Callender, Clarence N. 45
Cater, Douglass 40
Casserley, Julien Victor L. 49
Chandler, Albert Richard 46
Charlesworth, James C. 45
Childs, John Lawrence 61
Childs, Marquis William 40
Collins, Joseph Burns 73
Confrey, Burton 70
Conger, George Perrigo 24
Connell, Francis Jeremiah 11, 24
Cook, Elaine F. 50
Cook, Lloyd Allen 50
Coulson, C. A. 56
Cox, Lillian E. 69, 70
Crawford, Leonidas W. 62
Cunningham, William Francis 11, 73

Davidson, Robert Franklin 25
Dawson, Joseph M. 12
Demant, Vigo Auguste 41
Demiashkevich, Michael John ... 36

Department of Elementary School
    Principals (NEA) 65
Dewey, John 25
Douglass, Paul Howard 46
DuNoüy, Pierre Lecomte 57
Dracher, Norman 12
Dreikurs, Rudolph 31
Drummond, Henry 57

Ebersole, Luke Eugene 46
Eddington, Arthur Stanley 54
Education Policies Commission .. 81
Everett, Millard Spencer 25

Fairchild, Henry Pratt 74
Fairchild, Hoxie Neale 13
Ferré, Nels Frederick S. 13
Finkelstein, Louis 60
Finley, John Huston 80
Fitch, Florence Mary 66
Fitzpatrick, Edward Augustus
                        61, 66, 74
Fleming William Sherman 3
Fromm, Erich 31

Gaebelein, Frank Ely 14
Gauss, Christian Frederick 74
Gerhart, Eugene C. 47
Gilbert, Fred 66
Ginzberg, Eli 14
Greene, Evarts B. 44
Greenstock, David Lionel 62

Haldane, John Scott 58
Hallowell, John Hamilton 44
Hartshorne, Charles 26
Hartshorne, Hugh 75
Hay, Clyde Lemont 3
Hayes, Ernest H. 69, 70
Healy, Edwin F., (S. J.) 80
Hedley, George Percy 14, 75
Heim, Karl 55
Hennrich, Killan J. 70
Henry, Nelson B. 15
Henry, Virgil 15
Hocking, William Ernest 55
Hollingworth, Harry L. 32
Hosty, Thomas J. 71
Hoyt, Elizabeth Ellis 41
Hyde, William DeWitt .. 27, 67, 80
Hyma, Albert 47
Hudson, Winthrop Still 15
Hughley, Judge Neal 50
Hullfish, Henry Gordon 3
Hutchison, John Alexander 50

Huxley, Aldous Leonard 26

James, William 32
Johnson, Alvin Walter 4
Johnson, Frederick Ernest 4
Jones, Howard Mumford 36, 37
Jung, Carl Gustav 33

Kallen, Horace Meyer 27
Keller, James Gregory 16, 48
Kilpatrick, William H. 62
King, William Peter 33
Kirsch, Felix M. 16

Ligon, Ernest Mayfield 33
Link, Henry Charles 34
Limbert, Paul M. 75
Lippman, Walter 5
Livingston, Richard Winn ... 76, 81
Lotz, Philip Henry 62
Lord, Daniel A., (S. J.) 71
Lowry, Howard 17

MacEachen, Roderick A. 67
MacIver, Robert Morrison 48

McCollum, Vashti Cromwell 5
McDougall, William 34
McDowell, John Bernard 67
McGucken, William J., (S. J.) .. 71
McKinney, Richard Ishmael 76
McLean, Angus Hector 68
McMahon, John T. 76
McPeek, James A. S. 35

Madden, Ward Ellis 17
Martin, Renwick Harper 5
Mason, Frances Baker 58
May, Henry Farnham 51
May, Rollo 35
Meland, Bernard E. 29
Mill, John Stuart ....
Miller, Perry Gilbert E. 37, 63
Minister of Education, Ontario . 69
Moberly, Walter Hamilton 17
Morrison, Robert Bakewell, (S.
    J.) 77
Murray, Albert Victor 18

Neill, Thomas Patrick 51
Nelson, Claud D. 6
Neumann, Henry 18, 68
Niebuhr, Reinhold 44, 51
Niebuhr, Richard H. 6
Nottingham, Elizabeth Kristine . 52
O'Leary, Mary Florence Margaret 19
O'Neill, James Milton 6, 7
Ortega y Gasset, José 19
Osgniach, Augustine John 48

Painter, Franklin V. N. 19

Pfeffer, Leo 7
Pope Pius XI 12
Reed, Sidnell 70
Reese, William L. 26
Redden, John D. 20
Robinson, Daniel Sommer 27
Rogers, Edward 49
Ryan, Francis A. 20
Ryan, John Augustine 41
Russell, Bertrand 56

Sayers, Ephraim Vern 28
Scheele, Sister M. Augustine 38
Scheidlinger, Saul 35
Sherrington, Charles Scott 52
Shinn, Roger L. 45
Sinnott, Edmund Ware 59
Smith, Huston 77
Spann, John Richard 28
Stace, Walter Terrence 29
Stamp, Josiah Charles 42
Stokes, Anson Phelps 8
Sweet, William Warren 53
Syllabi, Religion, Agreed on for
    English Schools
        Cambridge 64
        Cheshire 64
        Exeter 65
        London 65
        Lincoln 64
        Middlesex 65
        Surrey 65
        Yorkshire 64

Tahon, Joseph V. 70
Tanner, Paul F. 66
Tawney, Richard Henry 42
Thayer, Vivian Trow 8
Tead, Ordway 63
Toynbee, Arnold Joseph 45
Troeltsch, Ernst 53

Van Dusen, Henry Pitney 20

Ward, Alfred Dudley 43
Ward, Harry Frederick 43
Walsh, Chad 77
Weatherhead, Leslie Dixon 38
Wieman, Henry Nelson 29
Wilder, Amos N. 21
Wilson, Karl K. 21
White, Lynn Townsend 77
Whitehead, Alfred North 56, 57
Wroten, James D. 8
Yale University Divinity School .. 9
Yeaxlee, Basil Alfred 81
Yost, Frank H. 4